Using Discourse Analysis to Improve Classroom Interaction

This accessible "how-to" text is about classroom interaction—how to study it and how to use that knowledge to improve teaching and learning. Actually *showing* what critical, constructionist, sociocultural perspectives on teaching, learning, and schooling are and what they can do, it makes discourse analysis understandable and useful to teachers and other nonlinguists.

Using Discourse Analysis to Improve Classroom Interaction:

- offers teachers the powerful tools of discourse analysis as a way of understanding the complex dynamics of human interaction that constitute effective, equitable teaching and learning
- guides readers step-by-step through how to build their **interactional awareness** to improve their teaching
- includes "Try It Out" exercises to engage readers in learning how to respond to the social dynamics of their classrooms for the purpose of improving classroom interaction.

Proceeding from simple illustrations to more complex layering of analytical concepts, short segments of talk, transcribed to highlight important points, are used to explain and illustrate the concepts. These segments of talk evoke everyday, complex dilemmas and challenging issues that teachers face in today's social and political environment. Method after method is unfolded to build the reader's capacity to use all the approaches together in analyzing the complexity of longer interactions. By the time readers get to the complicated issues addressed in the text they are ready to deal with some of teaching's toughest challenges—how issues of race are manifested in talk; valuing varieties of English and developing academic discourses; re-constructing resistant students as able ones; managing threats to teacher authority and legitimacy; managing relationships with colleagues; and negotiating institutional demands associated with high-stakes testing—and have the tools to build positive relationships among their students so that all can participate equally in the classroom.

Lesley A. Rex is Faculty Leader of Secondary English Teacher Education, Co-Chair of the Joint Ph.D. Program in English and Education, and Professor at the University of Michigan.

Laura Schiller is a National Board Certified teacher, Director of the Oakland (MI) Writing Project, Literacy Consultant for Oakland (MI) Intermediate School District, and University of Michigan doctoral student.

Using Discourse Analysis to Improve Classroom Interaction

Lesley A. Rex and Laura Schiller

NEW YORK AND LONDON

First published 2009
by Routledge
711 Third Avenue, New York, NY 10017

Simultaneously published in the UK
by Routledge
2 Park Square, Milton Park, Abingdon, Oxon OX14 4RN

*Routledge is an imprint of the Taylor & Francis Group,
an informa business*

Transferred to digital printing 2011

Typeset in Sabon by RefineCatch Limited, Bungay, Suffolk

Library of Congress Cataloging-in-Publication Data
Rex, Lesley A.
    Using discourse analysis to improve classroom interaction /
Lesley A. Rex and Laura Schiller.
        p. cm.
    1. Interaction analysis in education. 2. Discourse analysis.
I. Schiller, Laura. II. Title.
    LB1034.R49 2009
    401′.41 – dc22
    2008051501

ISBN10: 0–415–80113–3 (hbk)
ISBN10: 0–415–80114–1 (pbk)
ISBN10: 0–203–87698–9 (ebk)

ISBN13: 978–0–415–80113–3 (hbk)
ISBN13: 978–0–415–80114–0 (pbk)
ISBN13: 978–0–203–87698–5 (ebk)

For all the teachers and teachers of teachers who keep trying to improve their practice. You inspired this book.

Contents

Preface

This book is meant to help those of us who care about teaching and learning. It is for teacher educators and practitioners who have tried, often successfully, to improve student learning but who find there are still students—sometimes, whole groups of students—who are not successful in our schools and our classrooms. We are not suggesting replacing what is working. We are not suggesting we have the answer to all educational challenges. However, we want to offer ways to think about who is and is not learning and what to do about it.[1]

To assist learning, educators have relied upon technologies as simple as chalk and a blackboard or as complex as a computer. We all know that talk is a learning technology more integral to teaching and more essential than paper and pencil or electronics. Talk is key to classroom learning. It is the medium for constructing and reconstructing educational worlds such as classrooms and teacher learning sites. That talk builds and transforms knowledge is considered commonsense, but how talk builds knowledge through social engagement is equally important, though less obvious. Whether students or teachers learn with and from each other depends upon how they relate as they talk to each other as well as what they say and what they mean.[2]

Using Discourse Analysis to Improve Classroom Interaction is a book about how to build **interactional awareness** to improve teaching. A teacher who is interactionally aware understands that teachers and students act upon and influence each other when they talk together. Such understanding enables teachers to reflect upon how they create classroom conditions that encourage equitable learning. To assist in developing interactional awareness, we will share ways you can freeze classroom conversations for study to gain new insight into how language can become an effective teaching tool. We will illustrate how to replay these frozen conversations in order to understand the moment-to-moment interactions that support learning and learners or derail our best teaching intentions. Our aim is to provide you with a way of analyzing your conversations with your students. As your understanding expands so too do your choices for when to act and your repertoire of actions to take. You can improve your teaching and your students' learning, whether they are adults, adolescents, or children.[3]

The Inside Track

In this book, we will also use talk as a way to understand some of our most pressing teaching dilemmas. *Using Discourse Analysis to Improve Classroom Interaction* does not shy away from the challenging issues teachers face in today's social and political environment. These issues are not new. Concerns about policy, assessment, race, and ethnicity have been with the public schools since their inception; only specific contexts and their problems are unique. In the 1920s, teachers in those areas populated by increased numbers of poor European immigrants, such as New York, were expected to follow policies for evaluating, sorting, tracking, and teaching. Differences in race or ethnicity were common and testing was extensive. Under the banner of doing what was right and fair, the Stanford-Binet intelligence test, now discredited as culturally biased, was adapted from sorting military inductees in World War I, to sorting public school students. Though the historical conditions were different, race, policy, and testing were key interrelated issues, as they are today. White, middle-class women remain the largest percentage of our teaching force, especially in literacy. Cultural irrelevance remains a problem in curriculum and pedagogy for students of color. And, testing defines an achievement gap between students of color and their white counterparts, even allowing for socioeconomic status.

For over fifty years, researchers have studied teachers' and students' talk to gain a better understanding of how learning happens (Rex & Green, 2007).[4] Researchers have known that students are positioned through talk in particular ways that either open up or close down learning. But these understandings are not widely shared, understood, or applied in the teaching community. Researchers now take for granted that students who come from racially and ethnically diverse backgrounds often struggle in school cultures that mostly privilege white, female, middle-class ways of thinking, speaking, and acting. But understanding what that means in classroom contexts and how teachers should respond in their instruction is far from agreed upon.

Likewise, for the past half-century, researchers have studied curriculum as a way to improve student learning. In English/language arts we hear terms like alignment and authentic achievement, higher order thinking, reading strategies, writing process, or workshop. Teachers receive curriculum documents with standards, strands, benchmarks and expectations. They grapple with common assessments meant to align with end-of-course tests meant to reflect state curriculum objectives that privilege coverage over learning. Best practice becomes a cliché in the press of curriculum overload. How to make sense of it all leads some to cynicism, others to compliance, and others to close their doors and, to the extent possible, do their own thing. How do we get ahead of the deluge of curriculum mandates in ways that position teachers as sense-makers and students as learners?

In *Using Discourse Analysis to Improve Classroom Interaction*, we have made every attempt to address issues such as these that weigh heavily on teachers. Our central chapters take up the core issues of improving student learning, addressing difference, and making the most of accountability and assessment.

Classrooms and Teachers' Choices

Teachers encounter these difficult issues, such as accountability and cultural difference, when they interact with their students. These issues influence what teachers say to produce individual learning and whole class learning as a community. In *Using Discourse Analysis to Improve Classroom Interaction*, we show how the analysis of teacher and student classroom talk can illustrate how learning is built interactively. Group dynamics shape individual choices about what can be said, when, and to whom. Group dynamics also privilege and empower some while silencing others. By analyzing interactions, we can recognize that choices made at any point can alter possibilities for learning.[5]

Choices of what to say and when are related to who one thinks one is and how one wants to be perceived. All people, including teachers and students, need to feel a sense of their own importance and capability, and they gravitate toward others who signal, in the ways they talk to them, a recognition of their importance and worth. People do not want to participate in conditions where they feel devalued and powerless. We see disengagement when students resist classroom activity and when teachers decline to participate in professional learning communities. Social stability, essential for learning to go forward, depends on mutual recognition of worth and identity. Who one wants to appear to be, and whether or not that identity is recognized as productive for the work at hand, determines whether individuals will participate in building and sustaining a learning community.

In our teaching, teacher education, professional development, and research, we have noted that recognizing, or naming, unproductive choices is not sufficient (e.g., Rex & Schiller 2007).[6] Naming the problem does not solve it. **Discourse analysis** methods capture interaction in the moment, so we can look back at the discursive choices that were made, and consider what other choices were available. Often speakers think that what they do and say in any given situation is unique and original. However, discourse analysis over extended periods of time allows participants to see how their talk reoccurs in patterns. By looking back at what was said, teachers can imagine ways to disrupt confounding patterns to create more productive and equitable learning, so that everyone in the community feels powerful in relation to everyone else.[7]

Viewing Classrooms from a Language-in-use Perspective

To perform this kind of useful discourse analysis, it is helpful to understand how language performs certain kinds of work in classroom interactions. We call this way of thinking about classroom talk **language-in-use**. To see language-in-use, classrooms need to be viewed in multiple ways. These ways change depending on who is looking and for what purpose. For example, a principal may look at classroom management or teacher delivery of a lesson when she or he visits a classroom to conduct an observation. The teacher in that classroom may have worked to establish an atmosphere where students see themselves as writers. The principal sees some students writing, some talking quietly, and the teacher conferring with a student at her desk. The teacher is pleased with the full engagement of her students in the writing workshop, and regards what is happening as accomplished teaching. To her dismay the principal says, "I'll come back later when you are teaching."

A visiting parent may observe entirely differently. She is interested in her own child's work and not necessarily in the class workshop. She might be checking her child's spelling, grammar, handwriting, and behavior. Meanwhile, a student may be more attentive to what a friend thinks of his writing, or to the note the girls in the corner are passing between them. The principal, the teacher, the parent, and the student each take a different perspective on what is occurring in the classroom, which focuses their attention on some things and not others. They draw conclusions about what is happening and act accordingly.

Teachers, principals, and parents traditionally focus on what the students are physically doing and producing. They measure the abilities of teachers and learners through the behavioral and formal products of class activity—grades, tests, and student work. In this volume, we present a more complex perspective for understanding whether and how students are learning in our classrooms, by looking at the language-in-use. We study the interactions to see who can say and do what, with whom, when, for what purposes, and with what outcomes. We want to see how through talk knowledge is built (e.g., Rex & McEachen, 1999; Rex, 2001).[8] When individuals learn in classrooms or professional development settings, *what* they learn is intimately related to *how* they learn. This more complicated language-in-use perspective helps us know how to create opportunities for learning that are recognized by students and teachers.[9]

Who Are We to Do This Work?

We are classroom teachers first and foremost. Lesley is primarily a secondary English teacher, and Laura is mainly a K–8 English/language arts teacher. Lesley's experiences include decades in the California public and university school systems as English teacher and teacher educator. Laura's experiences draw upon years of classroom practice in an urban/suburban mid-sized school district in Michigan followed by years as a district and county literacy consultant.

We are both passionate about teaching and learning, particularly when it comes to students out of the mainstream. Lesley often recounts her experiences growing up in a working-class neighborhood in England where economic class greatly determined what one could achieve in life. In the 1930s, as expected for their class, Lesley's parents left school at thirteen and sixteen and, as Lesley says, "They couldn't read to me as a child because they were too busy working. I didn't start to value and read books until I reached high school." However, they promoted education, found places to live near good schools, and freed her time to focus on school. Lesley's perspective on education was shaped by her experience as an immigrant to the United States, always an outsider. This helps explain why, throughout her career, Lesley has advocated for educational opportunities for non-mainstream students, who often have limited academic access.

Laura's narrative is as a second generation American whose father benefited from the GI bill after World War II.

> My dad became a lawyer and his profession provided solid middle-class economic security for our family. I grew up privileged financially and academically and never questioned that privilege until my school district and neighborhood, where I attended school and taught, shifted from white to black. At a time when colleagues bemoaned the decline of the district, I was immersed in professional development through a National Writing Project site and found my students were achieving at higher levels than ever before. Their success was directly tied to my learning and I found myself advocating not only for my African American students but also for the transformative power professional learning provides for both teachers and students.

Drawing from Research and Experience

The interactions in this book come from our research and experiences in classrooms as far back as 1993 and as recently as 2008. We selected methods for describing these transcripts that show the complexity of social teaching and learning. The challenge has been to explain the complexity of classroom teaching and learning in ways that are understandable without oversimplifying. To oversimplify is to misrepresent. Yet to make things too complex can misrepresent through unnecessary complication. Our solution was to choose manners of representation and explanation we think you will recognize as "real" or authentic from your own experiences.

From our experiences we have built theoretical and practical understandings of successful heterogeneous classrooms. These are environments in which children who are at risk of failing or of being marginalized have successful opportunities to participate and learn. Some of the specific issues that have illuminated Lesley's work are tracking, mainstreaming of students with disabilities, and mixed race classrooms, mainly in high school English language arts classrooms. She has explored how race and class issues impact teaching and learning in the classrooms of White and African American teachers and African American students, and illuminated their cultural brokering practices. Laura, on the other hand, has spent many years teaching elementary school students and African American middle school students in a middle-class setting. With her current research, she is exploring teachers' understandings and applications of classroom interaction.

We have studied the effects of high stakes test preparation accountability on the classroom practices of teachers who were working hard to be inclusive. Lesley was able to illustrate the impact of national and local political trends on classroom practices which affect teachers and young people in counterproductive ways. In her professional development work, Laura worked to contain high stakes test preparation and reframe language around testing. Together, Lesley and Laura have extensive experience in a number of productive professional learning communities, including National Writing Projects. Our most recent investigations are of how disagreements can become productive in a teacher learning community.

In organizing this book, we had two purposes in mind. Our first purpose was for teachers to access tools they can use immediately to improve classroom interactions. The second purpose was to provide readers with resources to deepen their understandings of these interactions, without distracting from our main ideas. To that end, we have added text boxes that elaborate definitions, sources, and examples. We have also included endnotes for those readers who didn't want their reading interrupted with attributions they might not use. Finally, we have included what we call "Try It Outs," suggested ways you can experiment with what you are learning in your own context.

Through these types of information and the manner in which we convey them, we are making a statement about the value of classroom teachers, teaching, and the context of K-12 schooling. Teaching is intellectual work. It is no less demanding than building theory, analyzing research data, or writing about assertions for an academic audience. It is simply different. Teachers swim in data and conduct research, implicitly or explicitly, all the time. It is impossible not to do so while interacting with learners.

To provide discourse analysis knowledge that will contribute to teaching as research of one's practice, we have divided the book into four parts. Each chapter in each part builds upon the one before it. In Part 1 we lead readers through explanations of key concepts and analytical approaches. Part 2 deals with curriculum and how the concepts we present in the first part can help teachers make subject matter more meaningful to students. In Part 3, we take on the important issue of difference. We look at clashes and intersections between the different worlds of teachers and students, highlighting differences in racial and social worlds. Part 4 deals with accountability and assessment. We apply discourse analysis concepts as they relate to testing so as to create rich learning opportunities in the current testing environment.

In *Using Discourse Analysis to Improve Classroom Interaction*, we take on the gap between a half-century of language-based research on educational practice and its practical applications for teachers. Beginning with the actual dilemmas teachers confront in their classrooms, we explain how focusing on the way we as teachers talk with our students and on how they talk with us and each other is useful. Whether facing students who are disengaged or performing poorly, or integrating accountability measures into an already full curriculum, teachers benefit from knowing how understanding discursive practices can make a difference in their own and their students' performances. If when you finish the book you and your students are asking "How can I say this in a way that will forward the learning for the class as well as for me?" then we will feel our goal in this book has been achieved.

Notes

1 This book will best serve readers who want to improve how to prepare teachers to construct learning communities with their students and colleagues. Hundreds of books about how to establish learning communities are in print. Some provide a research-based overview of how to establish them (e.g., Morrissey, M. S. (2000). *Professional learning communities: An ongoing exploration.* Austin, TX: Southwest Educational Development Laboratory), and others, written by practitioners, advise from experience (e.g., DuFour, R., Eaker, R., & DuFour, R. (2005). *On common ground: The power of professional learning communities.* Bloomington, IN: Solution Tree). Many researchers have contributed to this large body of work by studying various professional learning communities (e.g., Grossman, P., Wineburg, S., & Woolworth, S. (2001). Toward a theory of teacher community. *Teachers College Record, 103*(6), 942–1012; Achinstein, B. (2002). Conflict amid Community: The micropolitics of teacher collaboration. *Teachers College Record, 104*(3), 421–455) and classroom learning communities (e.g., Bloome, D. Carter, S. P., Christian,

B. M., Otto, S., & Shuart-Faris, N. (2005). *Discourse analysis and the study of classroom language and literacy events—A microethnographic perspective.* Mahwah, NJ: Erlbaum), as have teacher educators (e.g., Sapon-Shevin, M. (2007). *Widening the circle: The power of inclusive classrooms.* Boston, MA: Beacon Press).

2 Knowledge about the importance of classroom talk and teacher and student identity has been available for a long time. In the early 1970s, Courtney Cazden, Del Hymes and Vera John disseminated useful ways of viewing and talking about classroom talk (Cazden, C. B., John, V. P., & Hymes, D. (Eds.). (1972) *Functions of language in the classroom.* New York: Teachers College Press), and Judith Green later summarized the research on teaching as a linguistic process (Green, J. (1983) Exploring classroom discourse: linguistic perspectives on teaching-learning processes. *Educational Psychologist, 18*(3), 180–198). They used the term discourse to mean spoken language in social settings like classrooms. Since their seminal thinking, a bounty of researchers, theorists, practitioners, and teacher educators have deepened the work in the area of classroom discourse. In this book we have extended that work to provide teachers, staff developers, teacher educators, and scholars of practice with practical, research-informed applications. To do so, we take on ways of looking at teaching and learning through talk. We will demonstrate key issues faced by teachers and teacher educators and illustrate ways of observing and analyzing each issue in actual settings. To make the most of these demonstrations, we present a view of teaching and learning that emphasizes spoken interaction. Our goal is to make visible, and accessible for teacher use, aspects of teaching and learning that can reshape classrooms and professional development sites into learning communities.

3 With this book we build on that bounty by focusing on actual classroom and professional development interactions to demonstrate how teachers build and sustain effective teaching and learning contexts. Our experiences as teachers, teacher educators, and educational researchers have convinced us that to be a successful teacher means being a successful observer, analyst and communicator of one's practice. Yet, there are few books for teachers that show them how to do so (Cf., Frank, C. (1999). *Ethnographic eyes: A teacher's guide to classroom observation.* Portsmouth, NH: Heinemann). Our experiences have also taught us that when schools educate well, teachers teach and learn from each other as well as with their students. Whether starting out, in mid-career, or after thirty-five years in the profession, successful teachers who enjoy the challenge of what they do, create and sustain successful teaching and learning among colleagues as well as with their students. Such teachers develop observational approaches and tactical strategies for engaging with their colleagues and students that recognize, respect, and capitalize on differences in understanding, beliefs, and styles. They have learned to recognize disagreements as opportunities. In this volume we present what we think are the most important dispositions, concepts, and skills for being a strategic and tactical observer of one's teaching talk, because what is said is key to keeping alive purposeful and meaningful learning for all involved.

4 Rex, L. A. & Green, J. L. (2007). Classroom discourse and interaction: Reading across the traditions. In B. Spolsky & F. M. Hult (Eds.), *International handbook of educational linguistics* (pp. 571–584). London: Blackwell.

5 We define learning communities in classrooms and professional development sites as a collective of individuals in relationships that form a socially cohesive group for the purpose of learning (Cf., Grossman, P., Wineburg, S., & Woolworth, S. (2001). Toward a theory of teacher community. *Teachers College Record, 103*(6), 942–1012).

6 Rex, L. & Schiller, L. (April, 2007). Alignment as disagreement and civil cooperation. Paper presented for the American Educational Research Association, Chicago, IL.

7 To apply discourse analysis to classrooms and professional learning communities so as to make patterned ways of talking and their outcomes visible requires a particular perspective. Language scholars refer to that perspective as language-in-use (Rex, L. A., & Green, J. L. (2007). Classroom discourse and interaction: Reading across the traditions. In B. Spolsky & F. M. Hult (Eds.), *International handbook of educational linguistics.* (pp. 571–584). London: Blackwell; Rex, L., Steadman, S., & Graciano, M. (2006). Researching the complexity of classroom interaction. In J. L. Green, G. Camilli, & P. B. Elmore (Eds.), *Handbook of complementary methods for research in education* (3rd ed.) (pp. 727–772). Washington, DC: American Educational Research Association).

8 Rex, L. A., & McEachen, D. (1999). "If anything is odd, inappropriate, confusing, or boring, it's probably important": The emergence of inclusive academic literacy through English classroom discussion practices. *Research in the Teaching of English, 34*(1), 65–129.

Rex, L. A. (2001). The remaking of a high school reader. *Reading Research Quarterly, 36*(3), 288–314.

9 The actions of the collective shape the individual member's opportunities for learning. And, each individual learner helps shape what the collective group values as worth learning (Green, J. L., & Dixon, D. (1993). Introduction to Talking Knowledge into Being: Discursive and social practices in classrooms. *Linguistics and Education, 5*(3&4), 231–240; Rex, L. A. (Ed.) (2006). *Discourse of opportunity: How talk in learning situations creates and constrains.* Interactional Ethnographic Studies in Teaching and Learning. Cresskill, NJ: Hampton Press). The students and teachers engage in social relationships co-constructed through interactions among individuals and the collective. Having the vantage point of language, beyond traditional measures, allows us to assume that all students and teachers are learners and capable.

Acknowledgments

One of the pleasures of writing this book in the way we have is introducing you to many of the teachers who made it possible. They speak off the page. By letting us harness their talk, our teacher colleagues have been trusting and generous with the gift of their own voices, and we are deeply indebted to them. Our choices of what to transcribe from the hundreds of hours available to us increase that debt because, as you will see, we have not always depicted them at their best, although there were smooth running and inspiring episodes aplenty. Rather we have often selected moments of missed opportunity, struggle, or undermining common to all teachers, in order to illuminate some of the fundamental challenges teachers, even the best ones, regularly face in talking with their students. We thank these dedicated and effective professionals for letting us put these moments under a microscope.

We cannot name them all but a few must be recognized for their contributions to our learning via their excellent work with students and colleagues. They are Dave McEachen, Jack Hobbs, Julie Martinez, Steve Bodnar, and Lyndon Coffey. Gail Setter, and the entire Literacy in Action study group that for more than a decade grew our thinking about discourse in professional development contexts, please know that these pages could not have been written without you.

We cannot recognize by name the K-12 students whose voices you will also hear, but we thank them for their enthusiastic support of our project. They gave our work life, even when it seemed more nosiness than research.

We owe many of our early insights to the Michigan Classroom Discourse Group (MCDiG). MCDiG, comprised of PreK-University educators, was formed at the prodding of Laura Roop, now Director of Outreach at the School of Education at the University of Michigan, who early on recognized the power of talk to transform how we think about learning interactions. Laura, for your friendship, mentoring, vision, and persistent belief in the promise of public education and social justice, we thank you.

Our work on high stakes testing owes much to Lucy Calkins, Founder of the Teachers College Reading and Writing Project and mentor from afar to so many educators, and to Linda Denstaedt and Judy Kelly. Both Linda and Judy are teachers of teachers *extraordinaire*. They set the standard for what it means to be a scholar of one's own practice and to learn for the sake of others. Thank you to all three, who continue to lead the field to deeper insights about teaching and learning.

In addition, we want to thank the University of Michigan English certification students who, in their Fall 2007 Teaching of English course, piloted an earlier version of this manuscript and offered feedback from their first encounters with discourse analysis as a new way to improve student teaching. Their enthusiastic encouragement and applications assured us of the importance of the book's contribution to practice. We also thank Ebony Thomas, our UM doctoral colleague, whose work with high school teachers included our book and provided invaluable feedback. Finally, we thank the Leadership Team for Literacy, an Oakland Schools collaborative that brings together teachers wanting to learn and grow their literacy practice. They read and responded to an early draft and saw in it the professional development potential to tackle difficult issues of race and class. Their response helped us view the book's possibilities from new angles.

To our manuscript readers who pushed for clarity, Linda Denstaedt, Kathleen Hayes-Parvin, Laura Roop, and Kristy Span, our thanks for spending hours rereading and offering suggestions. We owe you. And to our editor-at-large, Stacy Shultz, we can't thank you enough. You formatted, did final edits, checked our references, and made sure the book was print-worthy. Kudos. You helped us pull it all together, Stacy.

Part I

"Reading" Conversations, Opening Possibilities

For every complex problem, there is always an answer that is simple, complete, and . . . wrong.

H. L. Menken

Dancers must prepare for improvisation. That doesn't mean choreograph. It means know the music, decide which planes to work on, whether the surface, the floor, or flight. They've just got to know exactly what to do, and then they can improvise.

Nigel Lythgoe, *So You Think You Can Dance* (7.12.06)

Chapter 1

Talking and Learning

Ideal Classrooms Filled with Ideal Students

Teachers tell us that in a perfect school world, students would be engaged learners who respect one another, extend themselves to learn, do their homework, and earn high scores on assignments. Tension arises when one or more of these dream students falls short of our expectations.

A recent tense conversation with middle school colleagues may sound familiar. It's close to the end of the school year. Laura is meeting with a core team of department leaders and the principal. Here is what she remembers:

> We've co-planned staff development this year and are meeting to set direction for the next school year. Complaint fills our small meeting room. The gist of the conversation went like this: The staff are not interested in talking about professional development. Other issues have to come first. The list includes first addressing: rowdiness in the halls, students not putting their names on papers, pencils not brought to class, homework not turned in, students not in their seats when the bell rings, and students not reading and following directions. Before the staff are willing to talk about teaching and learning, they want to develop a consistent approach for handling student behavior.
>
> This conversation coincided with the school's need to decide on a new five-year cycle of School Improvement goals. Despite a year of studying ways to revise teaching to increase student learning opportunities and access to a rigorous curriculum, until student management issues were addressed, teaching and learning would remain on hold. As a staff developer, I was in a difficult position. From experience, I'd learned that when it comes to setting School Improvement goals, as soon as managing students trumps teaching and learning, the school slides away from a culture of learning to a culture focused heavily on control as a prerequisite for learning. We tend to get what we focus on. On the hot seat, in a moment of difficult conversation, I hoped to re-see the conversation as an

opportunity. If the teachers and I could ask a different set of questions, perhaps different possibilities could become available.

Reframing to Re-see Possibilities

Viewing teaching from a management **frame** is one way teachers "read" their practice.

> **Framing and Reframing:** A frame is a theory. It is a way of categorizing and seeing the world. What sense we make of a particular situation depends upon our frame of reference. Framing allows certain interpretations and rules out others.

It allows us to see some aspects of our instructional context. However, a management frame is not the only way to read what is happening in our classrooms and schools. Because Laura was familiar with reading or seeing teaching through multiple lenses, she was able to offer an alternative reading of the end-of-year frustration with student behaviors.

What if, she suggested, instead of viewing the situation through what *students* were doing, they read the situation from what *teachers* were doing? The lens, or perspective, shifted from student to teacher, leading them to ask different questions. They put up a wall chart with two columns: **Issues** and **Approaches**.

Issues	Approaches
No pencils No homework	Golf pencils Mailboxes for repeat offenders

They took each concern separately and identified which students they were talking about. They listed the issue and who exactly concerned them. Then, they listed approaches they could use or were using to address each issue.

It turned out that a majority of students were not causing a majority of the problems. Only a few students in each class repeatedly left their names off their papers. Short golf pencils available for the taking when needed solved the pencil issue. By identifying the types of directions students were not reading or following, the teachers thought of a way to scaffold complex directions by creating T-charts of **actors, actions, and effects.**

Actors	Actions	Effects

Even so, some Department Chairs continued to resist, believing that their role was to prepare students for the world of work and building responsibility was an important educational objective. Students not prepared for class should be penalized and the staff needed to decide on consistent punishment.

Not willing to give in with so much at stake, Laura acknowledged the concern and pushed for additional approaches. Most of the teachers decided what would work best with specific students. When they asked each other what they did when students were not in their seats, the list of effective approaches grew. By shifting the lens from student behaviors to teacher actions, more solutions appeared. Adopting an approach that shifted language from "these kids don't" to "we could try" promoted teacher agency. After a lengthy discussion, even reluctant Department Chairs agreed they could facilitate team conversations using Issue Approach Charts. The fraught conversation shifted from management issues to teaching and learning for School Improvement goals.

Why would **reframing** the situation from a student-centered lens to a teacher-centered lens ever have occurred to Laura in the heat of a difficult conversation?

She learned about reframing conversations from **discourse** analysis methods.

To **reframe** means to offer a different or competing interpretation of events, a different angle previously not considered.

Discourse: A discourse is a way a particular group of people interact with one another. Think of a discourse as socially communicative practices. How do we talk, look, gesture? How do we think? How do we write? What we know or do or say is constrained by the numerous discourse groups that influence and are influenced by our participation.

Every conversation can be "read" from multiple perspectives. In this case, the teacher perspective was focused on what the students wouldn't do. By realizing there are multiple actors in any conversation and knowing that those actors can be positioned in many ways, Laura was able to shift from the actions of the students to the actions of the teachers. Instead of "students can't," she rewrote the script to read "teachers could." Framing and positioning are central concepts in **discourse analysis**.

Discourse Analysis: The study of spoken, naturally occurring speech or communication.

Once we ask ourselves "who" is doing the action, we can imagine alternative **positionings**.

By shifting actors and actions, we can move from passive to active roles and open up new possibilities.

Positioning: Through conversation, people situate themselves and others with particular rights and obligations. Speakers take up or resist positions others create for them.

Have you ever used the phrase, "You're putting me in an awkward position"?

Try It Out: Reframe a Conversation

The next time you engage in a difficult conversation related to teaching, ask yourself, "Is there a way to reframe this conversation?" Think about who is doing the action. Could you turn the conversation inside out by asking who else could be an actor? Try starting with "What if . . ." and see if new possibilities become available.

Between the Ideal and the Real

It is widely recognized that the classroom teacher is the single most important factor in student learning. For decades, researchers have studied effective teaching and effective teachers. Richard Allington (2002) and a team of highly regarded researchers studied first and fourth grade teachers to determine why some elementary teachers are exemplary and get stellar results from their students.[1] Allington and colleagues identified time, texts, teaching, talk, tasks, and testing as critical features of effective elementary reading instruction. Time referred to the proportion of reading and writing students engaged in versus time spent on less significant activities. Texts referred to large amounts of successful reading throughout the day. Teaching was active and demonstrative. Tasks were longer and substantial. Testing was based on effort and growth versus achievement alone. When it came to talk in these successful classrooms, there was more of it and it was of a different quality from talk in more traditional classrooms. Questions were open-ended, answers elaborated. Beyond that, Allington recognized the need to study talk and to find ways to help classroom teachers create the kinds of interactions that support learners and learning.

Secondary literacy education researcher, Arthur Applebee (1996), agrees with Allington about the essential nature of talk to learning and goes even further, asserting that all learning is social and cultural and curriculum is enacted through conversation.[2] In *Curriculum as Conversation* (1996), Applebee offers numerous suggestions to teachers for creating classrooms that privilege knowledge-in-action. Among those recommendations, teachers should:

- provide instructional scaffolding (p. 114) that supports students in a classroom context to learn what they cannot learn alone.
- make tacit knowledge explicit.
- balance activities so they are not too boring or too demanding.
- mediate the social interactions of the classroom to promote access to an academic discourse.
- negotiate the numerous discourses students bring with them to the classroom from their home, peer, community, and national cultures, as well as the student's need for individual recognition and differentiation.
- structure curricular conversations to generate an integrated curriculum.

Had enough? Further, Applebee notes that classroom cultures differ and the same thing said in one classroom may have an entirely different meaning in another classroom. While brief examples are mentioned, I doubt most teachers reading these admonitions would have sufficient guidance to enact them. Certainly, Applebee sees the importance of discourse to learning, but teachers still need clear guidance on how to enact these sophisticated principles of curriculum as talk.

Adding yet another lens through which to view excellent teaching and learning is a large-scale study from the University of Wisconsin on Authentic Academic Achievement. Researchers looked at elementary, middle, and high schools across the country, focusing on mathematics and social studies, to determine the effect of authentic pedagogy and academic achievement. In their view, classroom instruction focused on higher order thinking, substantive conversation, deep knowledge, and connections to the world beyond the classroom. Substantive conversation was explained as "extended conversational exchanges with the teacher and/or their peers about subject matter in a way that builds an improved and shared understanding of ideas or topics" (Newmann, Marks, & Gamoran 1996, p. 289).[3] The researchers were able to demonstrate that classrooms that ranked high on authentic pedagogy also ranked high on academic achievement. Further, they shared examples of classroom instruction that promoted high academic achievement. But how do we, as classroom teachers, live up to such standards?

The researchers have been helpful in telling us what to do, but not so good at explaining how to do it. Particularly where talk is concerned, Allington, Applebee, and Newmann point to the importance of teachers asking open-ended questions that probe for thinking. But what else is there when it comes to talk and learning? How do we build shared understanding of ideas? Is it as simple as asking particular types of questions? We know it isn't.

Chapter 2

Assuming and Choosing

Making Sense of Teaching and Learning Through Discourse Analysis

In order to improve teaching and learning, we study language-in-use in classrooms and in teacher learning communities. In the give and take of ordinary conversations, it can be difficult to remember who said what to whom. By freezing interactions through transcripts, we can read and reread to form interpretations of events and meanings.

Earlier, we touched on the importance of reframing conversations by repositioning the actors. Let's add to that insight the tool of freeze-framing. In this case, we are going to **freeze-frame** a brief classroom conversation.

Freeze-frame:

1. A still picture in the course of a movie or television film, made by running a series of identical frames or by stopping a reel or videotape at one desired frame.

2. A vivid, motionless scene or image.

But, before we read the transcript, some caveats are in order.

Speakers often speak in incomplete sentences. Speakers often overlap one another. It can be surprising to read a transcript of someone's spoken words. The speaker may be highly educated, yet the in-the-moment nature of conversation may sound fragmented when transcribed. Think about all the movements, such as gaze or gesture, that clue us in to a speaker's meaning. Think of all the unspoken understandings implied between speakers. Speech is more than what is heard, so a written transcript of what someone said may at first appear awkward to the reader.

Transcripts can be written to foreground different features of inter-action. Some transcripts do include eye gaze and gesture. In this book,

---

Transcripts: Written representations of spoken language.

---

our focus is on spoken interaction. We ask: What happens between speakers in-the-moment? We are focusing on what is said, how it is responded to, and what is accomplished as a result of that interaction. However, our transcripts do not stand alone. We don't just eavesdrop on a conversation, jot it down, and assume we have the slightest idea of what is going on between the two people. Well, we could, but that would be unfair and possibly dangerous if we were to act on that interpretation.

Transcripts are only one tool we use to capture, relive, and re-see complex interactions between people. As researchers trying to under-stand what is meaningful to people in a classroom or workshop, we need more than transcripts. We need **context** to help us understand what the speakers mean. So we live in classrooms for months at a time, video- and audio-recording, and collecting interviews and artifacts of student work and teacher plans. The excerpts of talk we present in this book come from this kind of research. Even though we present them with the context stripped away, the interpretations we have made of these transcripts would not be valid without all that initial context.

In this volume, we will not be providing extensive context for each transcript because we will not be arguing for the validity of our interpret-ations, which has been done elsewhere. Lesley's original research can be located in the references at the end of this book. Instead, we provide only limited context with transcripts to illustrate ways in which language is used. Our aim is to show how transcripts are invaluable professional tools that allow teachers to slow down a moment and reflect on its significance in their particular contexts.

Transcripts can be professional tools for educators because every teacher can adopt a researcher's eye. Teachers live in classrooms, know their expectations and intentions, and know their students. Teachers who become aware of difficult or awkward moments can use transcripts to reposition themselves and their students toward more productive relationships. Transcripts allow us to make the familiar strange. They allow us to freeze-frame a moment, replay and reconstruct it, and in the process of doing so, open up previously invisible choices of actions.

A Freeze-Frame

We think you will recognize the following transcript as a classroom interaction between an English teacher and her students. By transcribing it, we have frozen it in time, so that a reader could read it more than once to think about what is going on, and what that means for teachers and their interactions when teaching.

Transcript 2.1

1. JAKE: My grammar messed me up.

2. KEVIN: Mine did too.

3. JAKE: I have bad grammar.

4. JOLENE: I hear you guys. Some of you guys were saying that the grammar is what messed you up. That is correct.

5. DAVID: I thought you were about to say "that is so wrong."

6. JOLENE: Some of you need to proofread better. I think we need to work on maybe some proofreading strategies that I'll think about and come up with so that I can work with you on it. I think that sometimes people even get a little bit, almost too, dependent on the teacher to proofread it, and you're never going to learn that way. If you're dependent on me to proofread everything for you, you're not going to be able to proofread on your own. I'm going to tell you right now that when you get into college nobody's going to proofread for you. You may be able to get a peer to do it, but chances are the teacher won't.

Does this moment seem to be a successful teacher–pupil interaction? As the teacher, would you have responded differently? What is meaningful and important to you about this interaction? What are you assuming about the teacher and the students and about their classroom?

We didn't give you any context, so you have to bring a great deal of your own experience in classrooms to bear to make sense of what is going on in this freeze-frame. Here is some background information about the actual event that might help you form an interpretation closer to what the participants would say is going on. The setting is an eleventh grade English classroom. The teacher's name is Jolene. She is White and middle-class. Her students are Black and mostly middle-class. Accessing standard English is a prerequisite for college. Jolene and her students accept that as a fact. The students have all said they want to go on to college. Most students in this urban/suburban mid-sized district are expected to and do go on to higher education.

Now read the same transcript a second time with this information and a particular purpose in mind. Our purpose in this reading is to read the transcript to understand how Jolene thinks about her students. What are her **assumptions** about her students?

Assumption: A proposition or belief that is taken for granted and treated as true.

How do we think her assumptions influence what she chooses to say and do? How do her choices affect her students? If we become more aware of the assumptions we hold about students or colleagues, we can consciously create space for more productive engagements by choosing what we say and how we respond.

Here is some immediate situational context: On a day when Jolene talked individually with students about their grades for their writing, she overheard Jake explain the reason for his low grade to his neighbor, and she spoke up.

Transcript 2.2

1. JAKE: My grammar messed me up.

2. KEVIN: Mine did too.

3. JAKE: I have bad grammar.

4. JOLENE: I hear you guys, some of you guys talking that the grammar is what messed you up. That is correct.

5. DAVID: I thought you was about to say "that is so wrong."

6. JOLENE: Some of you need to proofread better. I think we need to work on maybe some uh proofreading strategies that I'll think about and come up with so that I can work with you on it. Um, one thing is, I think that sometimes people even get a little bit almost too dependent on the teacher to proofread it, and you're never going to learn that way. If you're dependent on me to proofread everything for you you're not going to be able to proofread on your own. I'm going to tell you right now when you get into college nobody's going to proofread for you. You may be able to get a peer to do it but chances are the teacher's not.

What are Jolene's assumptions about her students? Jolene thinks about her students as particular kinds of people. She says, "I'm going to tell you right now when you get into college nobody's going to proofread for you." Jolene assumes her students will go to college and she let's them know it. She doesn't sugarcoat the need for help with grammar, an issue that can be touchy for White teachers of Black students. In fact, her response surprised David, who thought Jolene might reassure them that their grammar wasn't that much of a problem.

Transcript 2.3

4. JOLENE: I hear you guys, some of you guys talking that the grammar is what messed you up. That is correct.

5. DAVID: I thought you was about to say "that is so wrong."

Jolene then told the boys that she would teach them in a way that would make them independent. In one interview, David reported, "She tells it like it is." Over the rest of the semester Jolene's students responded to her directness and trusted her intentions of helping them become successful. When she asked how they went about their schoolwork, many of them gave her straight answers since they knew the answers would not count against them and that Jolene would use the information in targeting her teaching.

Many assumptions are operating in this interchange. Jolene assumed that with targeted instruction her students could improve. She believed they all wanted to go to college, valued fluency in standard English grammar to get there and beyond, and were motivated to work. In turn, the students assumed she understood them, cared about them, and would teach them what they needed to know. Similar assumption-laden ways of talking throughout the term sustained their relationship and their roles. The students identified Jolene as a particular kind of teacher, and she viewed them as certain kinds of students. They shared some common perspectives about the purpose of schooling and how teaching should work.

Many teachers wish for better relationships with their students, those "ideal" students we dreamed of earlier. Becoming aware of our assumptions about students and how those assumptions lead us to position students has much to do with student engagement and motivation. Students who view their teacher as someone who cares about them, holds them in high regard, and provides them with the help they need to succeed are less likely to act out in class and are much more likely to want to be part of a learning community. However, this makes something complex seem simple. It's not. Sometimes we think we know our assumptions about our students or vice versa, yet our words can give us away. We may be sending a message to students that we're not even aware of.

The same can be said for interactions among teachers, administrators, and staff developers. Laura provides another example:

> I was sitting at a table with two district curriculum coordinators. We were reading the evaluations from an inservice I had just done. One curriculum coordinator said, "Well, at least they want to know more." The other responded, "Well, that's a change." I cringed at the disparaging tone toward the teachers. The separation of "us" and "them" raised a red flag. There's no way that teachers won't sense that hierarchical positioning. If that is the point of view you come from, you will communicate that view in small ways that you may be unaware of. But rest assured, teachers will hear and feel them—in your tone, use of pronouns, and in the respect given to some answers and not others.
>
> Once I heard this conversation, a previous encounter took on new meaning. A teacher from the workshop approached me to request help with acquiring materials. I was pleased that she wanted to implement what she'd learned. She addressed the curriculum coordinator saying, "I was just asking if we could copy these materials. Can the district do this?" After she left, the coordinator turned to her colleague and said, "She's never satisfied, so pushy." Without knowing the background I was at a loss as to what she meant. But the later conversation gave me the impression that the coordinators' comments made sense from their perspective. They viewed teachers as only willing to do the minimum—no time spent outside of school for extra planning and learning.

In these two conversations we can see two occurrences. The first is the speakers' generalizations about teachers' interest in learning and willingness to learn. We also observe the central office speakers' denigration of an individual teacher's motives in her request for learning materials. Whatever happened to create these points of view in the speakers, we cannot know. But what we can see is that the assumptions they have created are being reinforced in their talk and subsequent action, which was to deny the teacher's request.

Try It Out: Become Aware of Assumptions

Jot down several assumptions you have about your students. Next, jot down several assumptions you believe your students have about you. You have all the credibility you need as a researcher. You inhabit your classroom, you know the context, the interactions, the subtleties. With your background, interactions have more meaning than they would to an outsider.

Tape-record two class lessons. Listen to the tapes and pay attention to clues that signal your assumptions about your students. How do you position them? Write down the exact language used. Listen for clues about assumptions your students have about you. Can you confirm or disconfirm your original assumptions written down earlier? What do you make of this?

When I read David's comment in the Jolene transcript, it immediately set off alarms. David expected something different from his teacher. When I notice a **frame clash**, something said that I didn't expect, my discourse analyst's antennae go up and I try to understand the source of that clash.

Frame clash: When your experience runs counter to your expectation.

Watch for clashes. Watch for little moments of interaction when something doesn't fit quite right. These may lead you to new insights.

When you can see how your assumptions about your students play out in your class through talk, then it is easier to see how certain roles and relationships become established. Once we see what we do through what we say, we have an opportunity to change what we say to reshape those roles and relationships. We can engage multiple perspectives of diverse learners. To do that requires purposeful and conscious observation through a perspective that allows for complexity.

When you can see how the complexity plays out in your classroom, you can act to disrupt the usual course of events and challenge assumptions about people and their intentions and motivations.

An Interpretation is a Choice

We expect that you may have different interpretations from ours. As we have said, one reason for those differences is that we have lived in these classrooms for extended periods of time. We were there when these incidents happened and observed them firsthand. In addition, we have spent weeks at a time living in these schools getting to know the teachers and their students. Our interpretations are not solely based on the words in the transcripts. Rather, we bring our understandings of the dynamics of these **contexts** to bear on what we think people mean by what they say.

Context: Context can be a social condition as well as a physical space. The classroom context can be a site of resistance to learning or a community of learners. A family's home can be a context for affection and mutual support or a context for competition and isolation. Contexts vary depending on the circumstances and the people involved.

In your own classrooms, it is possible that you have experienced situations quite similar to those we present. Consequently, you will bring that background information to the interactions. You will also bring your own beliefs, values, and dispositions that lead you to make assumptions about what is occurring. In classrooms teachers always make assumptions about the interactions they observe and engage in.

As you read, we encourage you to bring your own experiences to the transcripts as you follow our discussion. Recognizing similarities between your own situations and the classrooms in the transcripts will make the book more useful for you. However, since every reader brings a different experience to each transcript, you will inevitably find that you may disagree with our interpretations. This is unavoidable and, we think, good. Those clashes are places of possibility. That's where learning can occur as we ask you to notice your assumptions and try on our ways of seeing. Our view involves learning several discourse analysis methods for reflecting on important moments of interaction. Through reflection, we can open the possibility of choosing how we talk with students and colleagues more productively.

Interpretations Have Consequences

At the beginning of this chapter, we provided you with a particular kind of transcript that encouraged you to read and make meaningful some things and not others. We purposefully removed all the pauses, repeated words, and uhms and ahs, as well as false starts of sentences. We turned the interaction into conventional standard English prose so that it would read easily and not lead you to draw conclusions about the speakers based on the language forms they used. Linguists have pointed out that people draw conclusions about the intelligence or cognitive abilities of others on the basis of their language. Instead, we wanted to foreground the meaning you would make about the teaching and learning aspects of the interaction.

Let us revisit this classroom freeze-frame again in a different transcript form. This time we want to foreground potential learning clashes. Try one out. Read Transcript 2.4 below as a discourse analyst might who does the first of many reads of a transcript. As you do, keep in mind the following questions: What's going on here? What is this situation? Who are these people? What do they seem to value? What are their relationships?

Transcript 2.4

1. JAKE: My grammar messed me up.

2. KEVIN: Mine did too.

3. JAKE: I have bad grammar.

4. JOLENE: I hear you guys, some of you guys talking that the grammar is what messed you up. That is correct.

5. DAVID: I thought you was about to say "that is so wrong."

6. JOLENE: Some of you need to proofread better. I think we need to work on maybe some uh proofreading strategies that I'll think about and come up with so that I can work with you on it. Um, one thing is, I think that sometimes people even get a little bit almost too dependent on the teacher to proofread it, and you're never gonna learn that way. If you're dependent on me to proofread everything for you you're not gonna be able to proofread on your own. I'm gonna tell you right now when you get into college nobody's gonna proofread for you. You may be able to get a peer to do it but chances are the teacher's not.

Compare your interpretations with ours: Jolene is a teacher who has handed back papers, and three of her students are discussing why their grades were low. The teacher overhears them talking and agrees with their self-assessment. She says she will figure out ways she can help improve their grammar, yet warns them that they need to learn to proofread their own grammar because their college teachers won't do that for them.

Most likely you have ideas about what kind of class this is and who these students might be. If you keep yours in mind as we provide our interpretations, we hope you will critique your own as well as ours in what we intend to be a productive tension. Our goal is that the tension will engage you in understanding, using, and learning analytical methods that you can take into your own practice. It is not important to us that you believe our interpretations, although one of us was present when each interaction occurred. We have a firsthand understanding of the social dynamics of the people involved and of their groups. We have firsthand information that bears on what the speakers meant and why they said what they did. That information informs our interpretations; however, that doesn't make ours right and yours wrong. How we bring that information to bear on understanding what is occurring in the interactions through the methods of analysis is the learning we want to provide in this book. That means that it is better if you read with a critical eye.

Chapter 3

Interacting and Positioning

Identity

During a recent discussion about ways to improve adolescent literacy, a school administrator voiced exasperation: "We agree that comprehension strategies are necessary if students are to understand what they read, so why can't we just mandate everyone teach comprehension strategies and be done with it?" We empathize, but we also know that if we are going to improve student understanding, we are also going to have to improve understanding our students. And a productive place to begin is with identity.

> **Identity:** How individuals label themselves as members of particular groups.

Discourse analysis methods offer three concepts related to identity that are particularly helpful when working with learners, whether children or adults. The first is the concept of identities and relationships. The second is the concept of recognizing identities, your own and others. The third discourse analysis concept related to identities is how positioning affects identity. Understanding these three concepts is essential to successful teaching and learning, so we'll take them one at a time. Our aim is for you to become aware of these concepts and draw upon them every time you are a hearer or a speaker.

Identity: Relationships, Recognition, and Positioning

Think of yourself as a teacher in a classroom. Where are you physically? How do you sound? What are you saying? Now think of yourself as a colleague in a staff meeting. Do you sound the same? Do you speak with the same tone of voice? Where are you physically? The point is, you speak and act one way in the classroom where you are the teacher. You speak and act in a different way when you are a colleague. The relationships we have with people in different *contexts* influence the identities we present.

Now, let's go a step further. How do your colleagues perceive you and vice versa? What about your students? What do they think of you? Think of a challenging student. How do you perceive that student? When you're in a staff meeting, can you predict which teacher will usually disagree with the majority? In your classroom, is there a class clown?

Others recognize these identities because they are displayed over and over again. After a while, others begin to name those identities and associate them with individuals. The student who jokes repeatedly during class becomes known as the class clown. It takes repeated displays for others to recognize someone's identity.

The same is true for your students' perceptions of you. They recognize you as a particular kind of person by the ways you interact with them over time. The concepts of identities and relationships and identities and recognition are easy to understand if we apply them to a media celebrity. Take Bill Gates as an example. Gates' identities can vary depending on where he is and with whom he is speaking. He can be perceived as a philanthropist, genius, entrepreneur, computer wonk, visionary, or cutthroat business monopolist. What self he **chooses** to display and how others will recognize his identity will largely depend on his relationship with the hearers and where he is.

Choosing: Being aware of student identities and responding to those identities requires self-reflection. "If I say it this way, how am I positioning the student versus if I say it another way?" We choose ways to use language that recognize identities and selves in order to engage and affirm learners, particularly those who are most reluctant.

In less public contexts, teachers and students construct recognizable identities for each other, even if it's as "the silent one" or "the voracious reader." These identities may evolve within a single school setting or differ across settings. They can even change within the same classroom when the discourse patterns change or a member leaves or enters.

Choices of what to say and when are related to who we are and how we want to be perceived. Every person needs to feel a sense of their own importance and capability, and will gravitate toward others who signal, in the ways they talk to them, a recognition of their importance and worth. Jolene's students perceived her as a teacher who was honest with her students and would help them achieve their goals. Jolene perceived her students as capable of learning what they needed to know and, through her talk, she positioned them as college-bound students.[4]

People do not want to participate in conditions where they feel devalued and powerless. And we don't want to train our students to be passive toward powerful authority. We see disengagement when students resist classroom activity and when teachers decline to participate in professional learning communities. For learning to go forward, the mutual recognition of worth and identity must be present. Who one wants to appear to be, and whether or not that identity is recognized as productive for the work at hand, determines whether individuals will participate in building and sustaining a learning community.

Another transcript from Jolene's class demonstrates positioning that could evolve into an identity recognized by the teacher and the rest of the class. Jolene is conferring with John about a draft of his literary essay.

Transcript 3.1

1. JOLENE: You. No personal pronouns. Get 'em out, anywhere you find 'em. I found a couple, you may find some others. Awkward. (Jolene reads John's paper) "A good theme that can be used in book two, 'Flight,' of *Native Son*, is the concept of blindness." A good theme, how could you say that a little bit better?

2. JOHN: It was 2 a.m. when I wrote it.

3. JOLENE: Okay, well let's think of a better way to say that, 'cause you're a better writer than that. A good theme, come on . . .

If we want students to assume particular identities, then we must be aware of how we position them and what we say, which over time creates identities that students adopt. Let's look closely at this transcript.

Jolene, the English teacher, positions John as a particular kind of writer. John responds in a way that indicates he shares her view of his identity. By saying it was 2 a.m. when he wrote the draft, John provides an excuse for its inadequacies. The fault is in the lateness of the hour, not in his capabilities as a writer. When Jolene asks John, "How could you say that a little bit better," she believes he can answer that question. She wouldn't ask him to revise unless she believed he was the sort of writer who could do so. She assumes that this is an early draft and he can do a better job next go round. Jolene confirms this view of him as a good writer and accepts his excuse without question when she says, "Okay, well let's think of a better way to say that, 'cause you're a better writer than that." She will help him out, and even gently teases his performance.

This discussion of discourse displays a possible choice we can make as teachers. Jolene's positioning of John as a competent writer ("you're a better writer than that") and her high expectations for his work offer a way of thinking about how we position students in similar situations. How we choose to respond to students can contribute to making the difference between a student accepting or resisting the role and related actions you are asking him to take on. In that moment, if the identity you ascribe to the student in the way you talk to him matches his sense of self in that moment, acceptance is likely. However, if identity and self do not match, resistance is more likely.

We have found James Gee's view of identity helpful.[5] Students and teachers reinforce and reconstitute "selves" when they take on discursive "**identity kits**" or ways of being in the world (including gestures, clothing, expressions, idioms, and language) during classroom activity.

Identity Kits: Multiple ways of dressing, gesturing, walking, speaking, writing, laughing, etc. comprise each person's identity kit. These make it possible to present different identities in different situations.

Have you ever noticed a group of teachers at a restaurant? More often than not, without even speaking to them, you can tell they're teachers.

It is the same with students, particularly adolescents, who adopt dress, posture, language, music, etc. to be recognized as a particular kind of person.

Visualize the student who dresses in low-hanging baggy pants, oversized T-shirts, and backward cap. Or, think of the student whose grooming and wardrobe are always meticulous, right down to polished nails. We know that students "try on" multiple identity kits to explore where they belong socially. Does that mean teachers do as well? Think about the persona you assume with different classes of students or with the same class when classroom dynamics change. Jolene is a maternal encourager one moment and a commanding authority the next. Similarly, educators assume different identities with their colleagues depending on the circumstances and dynamics of the occasion. During professional meetings, one moment a teacher may assume her identity as a parent and share advice about child rearing, and the next she's a well-read children's literature expert reporting on a text she wants to have adopted.

Students and teachers position themselves in relation to others as they engage socially. Through their discourse they recognize themselves and others as certain kinds of people. These are ways of being in the world with instructions about how to look, act, and talk, so as to take on particular social roles that others will recognize. Understandably, those teachers and students who share cultural and social dispositions, beliefs, and values are more likely to have identity kit choices in common. For example, John, David, Jake, and Kevin share the identity of aspiring college student. As a college graduate, Jolene, their teacher, recognizes that identity and values it. Students who ascribe to ways of being in the world different from those required for classroom participation may struggle with issues of social membership and have difficulty demonstrating capability.

Try It Out: Evidence of Identity

Tape-record and write down (transcribe) a teacher–student conference. What evidence can you find that indicates the identity or self the student wants to put forward? What evidence can you find that indicates the identity you ascribe to the student? Does the identity you ascribe to the student in the way you talk to him/her match the student's sense of self in that moment? How can you tell? Should the student's identity not align with the teacher's identity for that student, what language choices are available to the teacher that might reposition the student?

Chapter 4

Identity and Worlds

Worlds

If we think of identity as ways of being in the world, then what is the world? Or, for our purposes, what view of the world is useful for our understanding of how discourse works? We already know that our country's ethnic, racial, urban, suburban, rural, and economic diversity means that most of us will teach students who are from different worlds from ours. What does that mean in terms of discourse and interaction?

In the following interaction, Nathan, a ninth grade English student, and his teacher, Marita, have been discussing his paragraph. Background that will help you make sense of this excerpt includes the fact that Nathan and Marita are Black and Marita grew up in the same inner city neighborhood as Nathan. However, Marita earned a teaching degree and moved out of the inner city as a young adult and into a middle-class neighborhood. You will notice that this transcript contains some additional marks in the form of equals signs. These are the first of several notations that will appear in the transcripts that follow. They are meant to show how the talk is spoken. The equals signs, for example, indicate that one speaker speaks immediately after another, which could indicate eagerness to speak.

> **Worlds:** Through talking, we bring our worlds into existence. My world and your world may or may not be the same. Teachers may never know a student's worlds. We must listen well to hear how students represent their worlds so that we are able to respond in meaningful ways.

There are many ways to write up a transcript. In this excerpt, we use the equals sign = to indicate one person's words following right after another's words. For example, when Marita said, That wouldn't be true though= Nathan responded without a pause and argued, =It is true.

In addition to the latching sign connecting Nathan's words with Marita's words, we also underlined is to show that Nathan stressed that word in his speech.

This type of information helps the reader form an interpretation of the exchange.

Transcription Conventions

↑	Rise in intonation
↓	Drop in intonation
: :	An extension of the sound to indicate a stretched delivery (e.g., wha::t)
[ ]	Simultaneous talk
(.)	Pauses of less than a second
(.2)	Pauses in seconds (e.g., 2 seconds pause)
=	Latching on of talk
< >	Rushed talk
xxx	Unintelligible talk
—	Underlining reflects emphasis through louder volume

Nathan is explaining what he means by his essay's topic sentence: *Drugs doesn't affect me and my family and my community.*

Transcript 4.1

1. NATHAN: Ok. What I'm saying drugs doesn't affect me and my family and my community.

2. MARITA: That wouldn't be true though=

3. NATHAN: =It is true. Where I live we say no to drugs.

   The whole community we all stay together and we are drug free 'cause we all are athletes.

His teacher, Marita, has many choices as to how to respond to his utterance.

> **Utterance:** A natural unit of speech bounded by breaths or pauses.

She could, for example, correct his grammar; ask him to use different words to explain his point; or, ask him why he thinks that is a truthful statement. Instead, she makes another choice and suggests that what he has said would not be true. Her utterance challenges his depiction of his world—his neighborhood, his community, his social groups, his family, and his church—as well as his identity as a member of that world. Her world is informed by her personal experience of growing up in the inner city where Nathan now lives. She has also read the reports of the effects of the drug trade on poor neighborhoods and on the futures of their young men, as well as the price paid by families. Her world may intersect with Nathan's, but is it the same? They share the same race, the same city of origin, and the same language. However, Marita's world is now middle-class, educated, and upwardly mobile. She has earned two Master's degrees, traveled, and moved into a neighborhood outside the inner city.

Our different identities, positioned in different worlds, influence what we may or may not say, as well as what we choose to say. Marita felt free to directly challenge Nathan's depiction of his world. We know from interviews with Marita that she was deeply committed to educating her students out of inner city life and into what she saw as more promising futures. Her challenge was for the best of intentions, but was it the best choice? What were the consequences? From Nathan's response we see that he defensively argues for his point of view. His identity, his motivation, values, beliefs and dispositions, and his purpose are under attack. Whether he resists or accepts the teacher's instruction depends on what she says next. His actions also depend on whether he perceives in her words that she understands his world and his identity in that world. Marita is more likely to select words that convey this understanding if she perceives what Nathan is doing—that is, if she understands why he is arguing against her challenge to his topic sentence. If she sees that his identity is on the line, she can respond in a way that backs off from her initial challenge. If the two of them have an established history of inter-actions that respect his identity, then the chances are good that he will continue to accept her teaching despite her affront. In the same way, even though John's paper showed little effort, John and his teacher, Jolene, shared sufficient positive prior interactions to sustain Jolene's confidence in him.

Try It Out: Capturing Moments of Interest

Set up a camera in your classroom closest to wherever you locate yourself most of the time. Perhaps you usually stand near the front of the room. Or perhaps you often sit at your desk when conferring with students. Decide the best placement for your camera so that it can pick up many of your interactions with students. Check the sound quality so that you can capture your voice and the student voices nearest you. Then turn it on and forget about it until class is over.

You won't need to replay the entire tape or disc. The chances are you'll remember a moment when it seemed as if you and a student were out of sync or in disagreement with one another. Find just that moment and transcribe a minute or two. It is possible you'll want to keep your camera on for a week. Just knowing you're capturing interactions will remind you of conversations to look for on tape that hint at a clash of worlds.

What do you notice? What discursive choices did you make? How did the student respond? What did you say back? How else could the conversation have gone? When you interacted with the student, did you honor his/her world and identity? What evidence for that honoring do you have in the transcript?

What else could you have uttered? Would the student response likely have been different?

Remember, students may respond by being silent. This, too, is worth reflection. What does the silence indicate? How do you know?

Chapter 5

Interdiscursivity

To put it simply, **interdiscursivity** means we all come from multiple worlds and when we interact through talk with others, their worlds and our worlds intersect and sometimes clash.[6]

> **Interdiscursivity:** Discourses do not stand alone. They intersect, overlap, and intertwine. Further, discourses operate in relation to or in opposition to other discourses.

Worlds, when seen from the perspective of language, are interrelated webs of discourses. Every interaction reflects all the discourses available to the **interactants**.

> **Interactants:** The people involved in a conversation.

One way of thinking about this multitude of discourses is that though they are readily available to speakers to use at any moment, we are not in control of them, nor are we always aware of the origins of discourses when we talk. We very often speak and only after the words are out of our mouths can we see the social effect of what we said. Another way of saying this is that sometimes our words seem to pull us along in their wake.

The values, beliefs, assumptions, and dispositions we have discursively taken on speak through us when we open our mouths. Our words stand in for and represent our worlds.

Marita is carrying multiple worlds that are discursively interrelated. She is part of a middle-class world that is shaped by her working-class childhood and her education; all those worlds speak through Marita. Nathan's worlds are also discursively interrelated. He is living in a working-class world where athletics are highly valued and drugs are talked about as destructive by coaches, mothers, and pastors. When

Marita talks to Nathan and Nathan responds, all their worlds intersect and create new meaning for both of them.

Try It Out: Investigating Worlds

Generate a list of as many of your worlds as you can name. Next, identify a person near and dear to you. Generate a list of as many of his/her worlds as you are aware of. Next, identify a person you find difficult to talk to or be around. Generate a list of as many of his/her worlds as you are aware of.

How do the lists compare? Where do your worlds intersect? Where do your worlds clash? What else can you say from this information? Have you been influenced by their worlds? Have you influenced their worlds?

Lesley:

When I try out the "Investigating Worlds" activity above, I realize that Marita and I have worlds in common. I am also the first in my family to go to college, and from a working-class family. My middle-class life has been earned through extensive higher education as well.

I also carry different worlds. I am a White woman born in South Africa, where my parents emigrated after my father served in World War II, and I was raised in England until my family emigrated to the USA. As my family moved extensively, I attended five elementary schools, three in England and two in southern California. My father left school at thirteen and became a linotype operator for urban newspapers. He was an avid union member, supporter of the civil rights movement, and left-leaning democrat who actively worked for political and social causes. As retirees, he and my mother devoted their free time to volunteering. One was to help found a Unitarian Fellowship, where as a teenager I learned to argue civilly about religion, philosophy, and politics.

I also know the worlds of hospitals and disability, having been born with a hole between the right and left ventricles of my heart. Open-heart surgery at thirteen changed me from a sickly, 95-lb child to a woman with permanent, but no longer life-threatening, disabilities.

I identify as disabled, immigrant, and successful navigator of schooling. Among other life stories, I am living Pygmalion's, so it's no wonder I regard discourse as key to mobility and success across national, social, and language borders.

Laura:

When I try out the "Investigating Worlds" activity, I recognize that I am a second-generation, college-educated, Jewish American. I grew up under the shadow of the Holocaust, with a father who fought in World War II.

I come from a traditional, patriarchal family where I was expected to marry, have children, and have a back-up job just in case. I was raised in a home that valued political participation, and I helped my parents campaign in local politics from the time I was two.

I grew up in the sixties at a time of rebellion, when elders and the political establishment were criticized for the war in Vietnam and racial discrimination, and women's rights were part of the national conversation. These worlds and more shape my interactions with others. At times I am aware of how my beliefs or values from these worlds shape my discursive interactions with others. At other times, my words come before my awareness. I am not always deliberate and conscious of my worlds when I speak.

Further, my worlds are always interacting with the worlds of others. Worlds are ever changing as they come in contact with new worlds. Until I attended a National Writing Project summer institute, it never occurred to me that teachers could have voice in the national dialogue about teaching and learning. This book, for example, is an outgrowth of that belief.

Practical Applications of Complex Relationships

The term interdiscursivity is useful as a description of the complex relationships among discourses that inform what speakers say. Every time someone says something it is influenced by multiple worlds and their utterance encounters multiple worlds. When we speak, we may not be aware of the worlds of meaning that inform what we say. Nor are those with whom we speak aware of the worlds that inform their hearing of what we say. However, whenever there is an occasion that calls for a spoken interaction, worlds will collide and intersect. At that moment speakers decide how best to speak so as to achieve their purposes.

Let us examine another transcript and the teacher's interpretation of the interaction to illustrate what we mean by interdiscursivity and how it plays a pivotal role in determining whether or not students will engage in learning. In the following example, Marie, a Reading Recovery teacher, analyzes an interaction with one of her students.[7] During the interchange, she had acted tactically to influence their unfolding discourse. She chose ways to speak that she hoped would keep her in alignment with six-year-old Danny and achieve her purpose of getting him to read a book.

Marie provides some context:

> The lesson before this was a difficult one—Danny was not engaged in the reading and the book he was to have practiced at home was such a struggle that it was clear he hadn't practiced at all. I had jotted a quick note to his mom to encourage her to ask him if we had met that day so that she would be aware of the days he had the extra reading assigned. Danny's mother took his progress very seriously, and I was a bit anxious that he and I might be at odds when he came in for this lesson because of the fallout. I was prepared to make any repairs needed to get our interactions back to pleasant, so when he came in wearing a team shirt with his name on the back, I seized the opportunity to show interest.

Transcript 5.1

1. T: Cool shirt . . . what do you like to play?
2. D: Inside soccer
3. T: Oh . . . indoor soccer . . . oh[good]
4. D: [my mom] . . um . threw away the note um . . cuz I did
5.   It
6. T: OK[good]
7. D: [but when I was reading xxx]
8. T: [OK lemme hear it]
9. D: "Dogs" . . . I really had trouble with . like . . the dogs . . that's the one thing
10. T: OK
11. D: "they help the farmer run up the sheep"
12. T: OK now . . . is it run up or round up?
13. D: Round up
14. T: What does that mean to round up?
15. D: It means like get them in a big group so the farmer can tell them where to go

16. T: Right . . . did you ever see the movie *Babe?*
17. D: The pig? Oh yeah, my mom loves that (big smile) and I love it
18. T: I do too . . . and they round up . . . remember Babe the pig could round up the sheep (chuckle)
19. D: Well . . . I don't remember that . . . but it's funny with the rooster . . .

At this point Danny is sitting close to me and I've swiveled my chair around so that I am completely facing him, undistracted by lesson records. We are as relaxed as if we were sitting at my kitchen table. He reads the rest of the book successfully, gives me a hug and goes back to class. We're back on the same team.

Marie's analysis:

Danny and I were chatting amiably about his sport (lines 1–3) when he brought up the note, telling me that his mom threw it away. Knowing his mom, this seemed difficult to believe, but I remained deferential and did not call this into question. I accepted that he read the book (lines 6 and 8). In the overlapped comment, line 7, he offered an example of a problem he had, adding credibility to his claim of having read it and perhaps offering in advance a reason that he might not read it correctly today. The book is about different kinds of dogs, so when he claimed to have had problems with only one thing, the dogs, it was quite amusing to me, but I did not question any part of his story. As soon as he began reading, I was more concerned with the content of the story than with his error (line 14). The sheep-herding dog reminded me of a movie that we had discussed many months ago and I asked him about it, seeking an area of common ground that I remembered was pleasant. When he responded to this topic, it was clear that the undone homework from the last lesson was no longer going to be an issue, and a struggle was avoided.

Because he was no longer in the regular intervention program, I had no pressure to keep records on his every move. This freed me to be really present to him and the result was a productive session that maintained not only his reading skills, but also our positive relationship.

This heightened level of consciousness enables teachers to surmise the worlds of their students. In turn, they can respond in ways that offer a better chance for students to relate. With this explicit consciousness, teachers can examine assumptions they form about students, assumptions that could limit options for interaction. Marie kept open the possibility that she could engage Danny, in the face of other assumptions about his truthfulness and his reading at home. When Danny first reported that his mom threw away Marie's note because he had done the reading, Marie chose to respond with *OK. good.* Later, when he explained that reading about the dogs had been difficult for him, Marie responded with *OK* to encourage him to keep talking, which he did. When next he mentioned that the dogs help the farmer run up the sheep, Marie asked if the words were *run up* or *round up.* Danny immediately identified *round up.* In this brief interaction, Marie had first chosen to position Danny as having read the book, even when she had doubts that he had. She continued to speak to him about his reading, which was her purpose. Marie is conscious of her capacity to choose speech acts that will have more likelihood of maintaining social relationship and alignment of purpose.[8] Both Marie and Danny wanted him to read the book. Danny knew that in the world of the school he should have given his mother the note, had her sign it after he had read the book, and brought the note back to his teacher. Danny's opening utterance indicated that he assumed this aspect of schooling procedure would have to be dealt with before reading could take place. Marie, conscious of Danny's move and of what, in school, typically occurs in situations such as this, chose not to give the expected response, choosing instead to focus on the reading. She chose to talk in ways that reinforce the relationship and Danny's identity as a reader.

Implications for Teaching and Learning

We now have a high school and an elementary school example of a similar situation, the kind of situation that occurs daily in our classrooms. In Jolene's case, her eleventh grader wrote his draft at 2 a.m. and did not work up to his capabilities. Of the many choices Jolene had to choose from, a common approach taken by teachers is to chide the student for last-minute, poorly thought out work and then either send the student back to redraft or give the student a low grade. Jolene did neither. Instead, she made it clear John was capable of revising his work at a higher level and she offered some direction. In doing so, Jolene and John remained in alignment. Both John and Jolene positioned him as a competent student, capable of better work. John blamed the late hour rather than his abilities and Jolene chose not to lecture him on last-minute work. John was then willing to revise and demonstrate writing more in keeping with his and his teacher's expectations.

In Marie and Danny's case, even at six years old, Danny knows what is expected at school. He was supposed to have his mother sign a note confirming that he had read a book for homework. Danny struggles with reading, enough to require a Reading Recovery intervention to help him catch up to his peers. Danny did not identify as a reader. If anything, he wanted to avoid reading and didn't give his mother the note as he was instructed.

But Danny knew what he was doing. He came prepared with an excuse about the note. He was savvy enough to concoct a reason why the reading was hard for him. In this way he thought he could prove to Marie that he had read for homework even though he didn't return the note. Marie's decision to align herself with Danny and focus only on what she wanted Danny to do – read – turned the tables on Danny's expectations. Rather than berate a child for a lack of responsibility, Marie positioned Danny as a reader. When Danny finished reading the book successfully, he felt good enough about the experience to hug Marie.

The importance of these two examples cannot be overstated. Both teachers broke with typical schooling expectations in order to position their students as capable and competent. Both John and Danny were clearly aware of what they had done, yet the teachers didn't allow either of them to adopt identities as unsuccessful writers or readers. If we think about who we want our students to become, then we can make decisions in the moment about whether we will focus on negative behaviors or reposition students as learners.

Try It Out: Being Positioned

Think of a time in your own schooling experience when a teacher positioned you as a learner or as an unsuccessful student. Do you recall the teacher's words? Do you recall your feelings? Could you describe this situation as a clash of worlds? What did you learn from the situation? How does it impact your teaching today?

Chapter 6

Power

Power

> **Power:** The probability that someone will be able to carry out his or her will though there may be resistance.

Power is an essential concept in discourse analysis. It is one of those touchy terms that make people nervous. People often think power means the right to control or have access to goods and resources. Those who think they have this kind of power want to keep it; and those who think they don't, want to get it. However, there are lots of other ways to think about power that are more useful for education. For instance, a learner can be said to have power when she or he demonstrates independence, ownership, or self-efficacy. The challenge for educators is to figure out how to empower everyone in the learning context. How could that work? And, if it were possible, what would result?

What is the difference, if any, between classroom management and exerting power in support of learning? For example, if when teacher Stan tells student Sonandra to step into the hall so as to manage her behavior, and she tells him she will discontinue the actions he finds problematic, is this traditional teacher power move an effective way to forward Sonandra's learning?

STAN: Step outside, please.

SONANDRA: OK. I'll quit it.

If we think about power as an individual's possession, then it is difficult to see how Sonandra has maintained any power in this interaction. Similarly, when a number of students exert their authority it is difficult to see how social stability and teaching could be maintained. Students with a strong sense of themselves and their right to be heard can overtake a teacher's lesson, whether in an Advanced Placement class or a remedial course. The desire for power can also lead to silent resistance and to nonproductive passivity, as common in professional development settings as in classrooms. Rather than thinking of classrooms and professional development settings as collections of powerful individuals, we take the perspective that for classrooms to be productive, power needs to circulate among members in a cooperative social relationship (Locher, 2004).[9]

We choose to take a different stance toward power. Rather than talking about classrooms and professional development settings as collections of powerful individuals, let us think about power in a way that maintains relationships, sustains conversations, and builds new knowledge. Imagine power circulating among members of a group who are interacting with one another.

Circulating social power for learning is analogous to the electrical current that comes out of wall sockets. Like social power, AC or alternating current is invisible. It is actually made up of electrons moving in alternating directions—sometimes going forward and sometimes going backwards—that generate energy. We think this movement of the electrons is comparable to the movement of energy between teachers and learners who are working together. Interest, focus, persistence, awareness, engagement, and enthusiasm are all invisible but essential electrons of energy that keep learning going. Just as you can't separate electrical energy from the light emitted from a lamp, you can't separate qualities such as interest and enthusiasm from learning. When you turn off the electricity or interest, the light and learning stop.

In a classroom or professional development setting, power is exchanged through social interaction. Power moves among speakers as they engage in learning.[10] To clarify the circulation of power in group learning situations, we will analyze three related transcripts. Once again, we will provide background that will help you read and we offer an interpretation of the transcripts.

The setting is the third session of an ongoing professional development workshop for high school English teachers. Lesley is the facilitator. The teachers in the workshop were expected to try out an activity on **stance**, having their students write from a particular stance or perspective about something they were reading in class.

Stance: Assuming a position or a point of view. In this case, students were learning how to take different stances related to their reading.

The teachers were expected to bring back the results to share with their colleagues. The discussion that followed one teacher's sharing gave everyone an opportunity to make connections to their own practice.

Gloria bravely volunteered to share her experience with the stance activity.

Transcript Conventions

In this transcript [brackets] indicate overlapping speech. Both speakers are talking at the same time.

Colons: are used to indicate the stretching out of a word.

Also, when you see [xxx] each x represents a syllable that was unintelligible on the tape.

Finally, this transcript breaks lines at the end of each intonation unit. When you listen to speech, you'll notice that phrases are separated by intonation—whether one's voice goes up or down helps the listener identify an intonation unit. It's not the same as a clause. Some transcripts are written as paragraphs of thought. This transcript is written in spoken phrases.

We say "bravely" because Gloria is a social studies teacher, who, after twenty-eight years of teaching social studies, was assigned to teach English. She volunteered to share her teaching homework with the group of more experienced English teacher colleagues, including English department chairs from two high schools, because she recognized an opportunity to receive constructive feedback.

Everyone knew this was Gloria's first year as an English teacher. However, whether a teacher is a veteran or a novice, sharing teaching and student work in front of colleagues is a risky business. Critique of teaching or critique of student work reflects back on the teacher's identity. Is this teacher competent and knowledgeable? Is she effective with students? To share student work is to share who we are as teachers, warts and all. Such sharing runs counter to established norms of practice. More often, teachers work in isolation from one another, the result of long-established traditions of schooling, separate classrooms, and norms of individualism. Even so, cadres of teachers and school reforms counter isolationist practices through professional learning communities and shared practice—an issue we will take up shortly.

As Gloria explained her classroom experience with stance it became apparent she misunderstood the concept. She had asked her students to take a stance about a poem the class read, and it seemed that her students had done so, as they became angry about the events described in the poem. But it also became clear as Gloria explained what she asked her students to do that she was confusing "stance" with "tone," fundamental concepts in literary analysis. The tone of a poem can be interpreted as the poet's stance or attitude toward the subject of the poem; whereas Gloria's assignment was to assist her students in taking their own stances toward the poem. Gloria's confusion is understandable for a teacher not well versed in her subject matter. Nevertheless it was a misunderstanding that needed to be pointed out.

Lesley didn't want Gloria to feel embarrassed or demeaned in front of the group. In the transcript, notice that Lesley initially said, "If you've got," then realized that would put Gloria in an uncomfortable position, and changed from "you" to "kids." By referring to the "kids" rather than to Gloria, Lesley deflected attention away from Gloria's practice and focused on what the kids needed to do. Lesley thought this repositioning move would make it more likely that Gloria would feel less threatened when Lesley conveyed the meaning of stance. By taking some of the pressure and focus off of what Gloria had done in class, Lesley assumed she could increase the likelihood of Gloria accepting new ideas.

Transcript 6.1

LESLEY: Sort of talk through

If you've got

And what we want <u>kids</u> to do is to take a

Stance because they really engage with the literature

In a way that they get hot about right

So you've got some kids here who are angry

Is it possible to take a stance on these texts

That that allows for anger in the stance and

That they can then go back into the text

And pull some evidence for

How there's stuff in the text that fu:els the

Righteousness of this anger

I think you could write that

TEACHERS: [Yes

[Oh yeah

LESLEY: so that the trick would be to

How do you finesse that

[Right

GLORIA: [Ri:ght

If it were just Lesley and Gloria alone, as it had been for Marie and Danny, the risk for Gloria would be far less. But in front of her colleagues of equal and greater status, the risk was higher. The higher the risk, the more careful the speaker should be when talking with the one in jeopardy. Additionally, Lesley had aims for the interaction beyond saving Gloria embarrassment. Concerned that Gloria might not want to continue in the group, she wanted Gloria to experience **self-efficacy** from collegial recognition.

Self-efficacy: The belief that one is capable and has the power to produce a desired result.

To publicly experience power meant that Gloria had to be **agentive** and re-establish herself as a competent English teacher in front of her colleagues.

Agentive: When a person takes action(s) regardless of outside constraints.

Transcript 6.2 presents an interaction that occurred a few minutes later. It demonstrates how Lesley attempted to circulate power to Gloria by building Gloria's example up in front of the other teachers. Just prior to this excerpt, Lesley had explained to Gloria what is meant by stance and Gloria had offered an example that indicated she was closer to understanding, but still not quite sure. Lesley began this next excerpt by naming and affirming Gloria's example as "a stance" and listing to the group the qualities of a strong stance in Gloria's answer. The affirmation of the characteristics of a stance Gloria had provided was meant to offset her previous misunderstanding and loss of status.

Transcript 6.2

LESLEY: Now that's a stance

[That's a wonderful stance

GLORIA: [I knew there was something in one of them

That we never learn from history

Because Claude McKay now has to say the sa::me thing

LESLEY: That's where we wanted to go

Right

Notice that it pulls all of the elements

That we wanted (.)

Engagement with the text

Pa:ssion

Stance

Evidence of a level of sophistication of tho:ught

That moves across the two texts

However, it is one thing for Gloria to be corrected by the facilitator, with whom she does not have a social relationship. It is more difficult for a colleague to critique Gloria's understanding. The closer in status, the greater the social threat.

So, when Ceil, a reading clinician in the group, picked up Lesley's move of focusing on Gloria's students, power circulated back to her. As a reading specialist with years of professional education, Ceil had high professional and social status in the group. This social identity made it more acceptable for her to try to teach Gloria. Nevertheless, an experienced group facilitator herself, Ceil was also conscious that what she said and how she said it could either alienate Gloria from the group or position her in a way that would facilitate new learning.

In this excerpt, observe Ceil hesitate as she searches for words. As an experienced English teacher she recognizes why Gloria's students were probably confused when Gloria conflated the concepts of "tone" and "stance." Ceil's purpose in the interaction was to explain the problem so that Gloria could understand how to improve her teaching and the overall purpose of the activity, without publicly threatening Gloria's status. Unsure of the success of her attempt, Ceil calls for help from the rest of the group.

Transcript 6.3

LESLEY: And what we want kids to do is to take a

CEIL: Umm I I as you were as you were talking

I think that probably uh the kids

Had a little bit of confusion ab:out uh

Talking about the poem and the to:ne

Which can be slightly different than taking a very specific sta:nce u:sing a tone[tone as <u>part</u> of the stance

TEACHERS: [uh-huh (nods)

CEIL: A tone

But but where I think probably in your student writing as you saw more of a dis<u>cuss</u>ion

Rather tha:n an argumen<u>ta</u>tion about here's directly how I feel and wh:y

So maybe the principle is that uh

Kids need to have a clear understa:nding of

Taking a specific stance

>I don't know

Help me with this<

   In the ways they talked to her, Lesley and Ceil attempted to position Gloria to reassume the power that she gave up when she allowed herself to be used as a teaching example. They were concerned with maintaining relationships, sustaining conversations, and building new knowledge They took the information that Gloria offered as an opportunity for everyone in the group to learn from Gloria's experience, directed potential open criticism away from Gloria, and fostered a circulation of power that they hoped would contribute to the development of a professional learning community.

Professional Learning Communities

Professional learning communities increasingly are advocated as the means for sustaining in-service teacher learning. Through analyzing interactive discourse, viewing the interpersonal social dynamics involved in creating and sustaining those communities becomes possible.

Understanding the social dynamics of a group provides avenues for interactants to make choices at any point to alter the way the dynamics are developing.

In her professional group, members made it possible for Gloria to experience this social energy, or form of **circulating power**, as self-efficacy, aligned purpose, identity recognition, personal and common understanding, shared assumptions, and meaningful choice.

Circulating Power: Learners' power in support of their learning may be thought of as independence, ownership, and self-efficacy. Power is not a possession. It circulates within the social conditions in which a person is acting. It's a movement of energy between teachers and learners who are working together. Interest, focus, persistence, awareness, engagement, and enthusiasm are essential energy generators that keep learning going. Interest and self-efficacy, and therefore learning of individual students (and teachers), require continual refreshing.

Gloria's self-efficacy can be seen in the excerpt that follows. Her words indicate that she appears comfortable enough with the group to poke fun at herself and to get everyone laughing with her. Her humor can be read as her sense of herself as realigned with the group as a capable member. For that moment, her identity as a competent English teacher is re-established. Through earlier utterances, Gloria has achieved personal understanding of the constructs at hand and the group has clarified their own understandings as well. The group has built shared assumptions about their learning—that we learn with and from each other by asking authentic questions about our practice and by revealing our practice to one another. Further, by the giving up and taking on of power in a discursive dance, we can make meaningful language choices that minimize embarrassment and facilitate ongoing learning.

Transcript 6.4

GLORIA: I'm glad my mistakes provided such a good lesson for al[l of you

ALL TEACHERS: [laughing

FACILITATOR: [Oh no

ALL TEACHERS: [laughing

FACILITATOR: I don't think they're mistakes

I mean we

When we're teaching

We're we never know what's going to happen right

And so we deal with whatever students present us with

The conditions of self-efficacy, aligned purpose, identity recognition, personal and common understanding, shared assumptions, and meaningful choice are what comprise community, and what it is possible to see and work with through discourse analysis.

Discourse analysis can make traditional definitions of community, that refer to trusting relationships, cooperation, and collaboration, accessible by illustrating how they can be talked into being.

Telling teachers to increase collaboration in their classrooms is not sufficient; we need to understand how to align with students in a way that will make collaboration more likely. In the same way, telling us that our classroom lacks trusting relationships is not productive. It names the problem but not how to solve it. To be able to act productively to change the situation, we need to understand how to see the worlds in which we and our students have invested identities and the assumptions guiding the discursive choices we have available to us.

Beyond individual power is the importance of thinking of power as a social resource. A social view of circulating power allows us to ask: How is classroom social stability maintained so that learning can go forward together, and so that learners feel the power of their own learning? From this perspective, a teacher's goal of everyone learning in her classroom is achieved by fostering norms for collective identity and knowledge co-construction. These norms forward a sense of community in which everyone feels powerful in relation to each other.

Social Stability: Social stability exists in classrooms, when collective identity and knowledge co-construction lead to a sense of community in which everyone feels powerful in relation to each other.

Try It Out: Circulation of Power

Observe an instance of power exchanged through social interaction. The context may be a staff meeting, a professional learning situation, or a department/team meeting. Are you able to notice the circulation of power?

Try to describe what you notice. You might pay attention to any of the following: (1) Who assumed a powerful stance, who relinquished power? (2) How were decisions arrived at? (3) Was there a tense moment when the group's social equilibrium was at stake? What did you notice about the circulation of power during that exchange? (4) How was equilibrium re-established?

If you were able to see power being exchanged from one speaker to another, what might this mean for you when you interact with others?

Laura:

When I try out this activity I remember my difficulties with mathematics. From fourth grade on, I struggled with math. I'll never forget my tenth grade geometry teacher berating me in front of the class for complaining about geometry to my counselor and then not finishing my homework. My friends in the class sympathized with me and I was angry with my teacher. My identity as a poor math student was reinforced and I didn't know where to turn for help. The power was in the hands of my teacher. I was powerless, hurt, and resentful.

I believe my desire to scaffold students' learning so they can be successful derives from my own struggle with math.

Lesley:

I'm dissatisfied with any social interaction I have in which I can't see power circulating. I've found that I get better service from the checkout person at the supermarket when she experiences how efficiently she's able to ring up my shopping. More people volunteer to share the load I'm carrying, from groceries to transferring bank accounts to teaching to writing books.

I'm quickly aware of those situations when I'm unsuccessful. I don't get on flights quickly after I'm delayed; the technology specialist can't seem to solve my computer problem; and, everybody is too busy to attend the meetings I call.

Saving Face

Another way of analyzing the social dimensions of the interactions we have presented is through the concept of **saving face**.

Saving Face: Protecting someone's view of himself or herself so they are not embarrassed or diminished in any way.

Have you ever felt the sting of a rebuke, or the embarrassment of having said the wrong thing at the wrong time? That is what discourse analysts refer to as a threat to your face, or to your sense of social prestige, respect, or self-assurance (Brown & Levinson, 1987; Goffman, 1967; O'Driscoll, 1996).[11] A threat to your social face is a threat to your ability to feel powerful in that social world. When you feel embarrassed, anxious, or defensive because of what someone has said, that is one indication that your face has been threatened. In order to sustain our sense of efficacy in a social situation, we need to feel that we have saved face. That requires the intervention of someone in that social circle. It could be the speaker who threatened our face, or it could be an overhearer who comes to our rescue.

Every person needs to feel a sense of their own importance and capability, and they gravitate toward others who signal in the ways they talk recognition of their importance and worth. You may have noticed that in any sustained teacher learning community, some members stay for the duration, and others stop attending, often without fanfare. A look at their social histories with the other members of the group may reveal why. Teachers stay engaged in professional learning groups with those who avoid intentionally threatening their face and step up to save it if necessary. And, teachers disengage from those social groups who don't. They may say that they are too busy to continue, but, often, that the busiest of teachers make time when they feel welcomed, valued, and productive in a social learning group.

Teachers and students alike recoil from threats to their faces. They can come to see the advantages of extending face-saving moves to those with whom they have invested social relationships. The dynamic and the work are the same in social situations as in classrooms. To build a learning community requires the conscious exercise of face saving to mitigate face-threatening acts. If we could always preview what we say before we say it, we could stop ourselves from uttering face threats. But that is not humanly possible, even for the most careful speakers among us. So we need to retrospectively assess what we have said, that is, after we have said it. In order to determine if we have threatened our listener's face, we should focus not only on what we meant, but even more on the listener's reaction. If we see distress, embarrassment, surprise, hesitation, or any of a number of similar responses, we **repair** (Iles, 1996; Liebscher & Daileyocain, 2003).[12]

> **Repair:** If we notice that we've made someone uncomfortable by something we've said, we will repair the situation by saying whatever we think will be best to help the person re-experience social respect.

Since teachers come from different worlds, in-the-moment slights are inevitable occurrences. How we negotiate clashes that mark deeper divides is a key and important element of the work of discourse analysis. In the remainder of the book we will provide illustrations of teachers engaged in this work, and offer ways of assessing and redressing what they are doing that could apply to your contexts.

Let's look at how Jolene, our high school English teacher, handled a clash between two students, Ben and Rena. When you read the transcript below, you will note that Ben experiences a social face threat from Rena. Even though Ben meant to joke, Rena, who also frequently vies for the class's attention, dismisses his humor with *That's stupid*. Jolene comes to Ben's rescue by sizing up the situation and repairing: *What's wrong with that? That might make a great story*, Jolene says in response to Rena, and, of course, to the class.

Transcript 6.5

JOLENE: How many people have no idea what they want to write about?

BEN: I'm going to write about how the blue bear ate the lunch box.

          (All students laugh)

RENA: That's stupid

BEN: I'm just playing.

JOLENE: What's wrong with that? That might make a great story.

In offering her repair Jolene achieved three objectives: she repositioned Ben so that he could save face, and she continued with her writing lesson. She also rebalanced the class's social equilibrium by defusing the social duel between Rena and Ben. How teachers handle clashes has a great deal to do with how students perceive their teacher. Is she fair? Does he relate to the students? Do students want to do their best for this teacher? Whether and how teachers repair social breaches and return balance and focus to learning is a key classroom social management tool.

Whose Face is Being Threatened?

In a different classroom, Ben's response to Jolene's question might have been read by the teacher as a threat to her authority—to the seriousness of her question: *How many people have no idea what they want to write about?* But not in this case. Jolene read Ben's remark as part of the tug-of-war for social attention between Ben and Rena, which she recognized as part of a social pattern. This pattern continued throughout the semester, and Jolene managed the social tugs-of-war between Ben and Rena by letting them unfold and then recognizing the interactions in positive relation to the curriculum of the moment.[13] Novice teachers, in particular, will benefit from the understanding that students engage socially with one another, vying for identity recognition and social status. If teachers make the mistake of assuming the student is challenging their authority and respond in that manner, the class recognizes the misreading and often will side or align with the student whose actions and intentions have been misread. Of course, there are exceptions to this, such as when a class doesn't like the student in question or when the teacher is very popular with the class. But, in general, it is best for teachers to be aware of the many motivations for student discursive interactions, and to avoid immediately setting up a confrontation.

Jolene's approach may seem counterintuitive for classroom management. Disciplining students when this behavior first appears is traditionally regarded as necessary to keep it from getting out of hand. However, our research in numerous classrooms of actively social students and their successful teachers suggests that the approach taken by teachers like Jolene is more effective in keeping students engaged in learning. Incorporating social relationship building into curricula activity is another means of circulating power in a way students recognize.

> **Face Threat:** An utterance or move that threatens a person's sense of herself and diminishes her status.

Face Threats: Adult versus Student Learners

In some situations in the classroom, such as with Ben and Rena, some group members may compete for social dominance. On the other hand, a dominant norm in adult professional development settings is to avoid potentially face-threatening topics and to be collegial when another member is challenged by an authority figure.

Transcription Conventions

There are three new conventions in these transcript excerpts. The up ↑ and down ↓ arrows indicate voice inflection. If a speaker's voice pitch goes up at the end of a line, it can indicate a questioning tone. Other times, depending on context, a raised pitch can indicate affirmation or agreement or can be a way of trying to align with other interactants.

When pitch drops at the end of a line it suggests closure or finality. It is a signal for the end of a unit of meaning.

Intonation meaning is always interpreted in the context of a broader conversation. In the case of these transcripts, the arrows were used only when the pitch change was emphasized by the speaker. In Transcript 6.1, when Gloria responded to Lesley's question, [Right↑, the tone she used, [Ri:ght↓, appeared to indicate uncertainty.

Another convention used in the transcripts is the elongation of parts of words. For example, in Transcript 6.3, when Ceil was speaking, she slowed her words, spacing out *ab:out* and *to:ne* and *sta:nce*. In this case, Ceil was hedging, trying to choose just the right words so she wouldn't embarrass Gloria by critiquing her teaching. Ceil's hedging was indicated by more than her drawing out of words. She also used words that indicated hesitancy, such as *but, but*, and *I think*, and *probably*. Interpreting transcripts requires reading for patterns that together warrant or strongly suggest a case or interpretation.

Finally, the third convention is the use of the greater than and less than signs. They indicate speeded up speech:

>I don't know

Help me with this<

Ceil rushes her words when she appeals to her colleagues to find face-saving ways to correct Gloria.

Collegiality often means avoiding and/or protecting oneself and one's colleagues from personal discomfort. Consequently, it is difficult to engage teachers in substantive sharing and examination of their practice.

When teachers come together to learn, because so often their personal identity is closely associated with their teacher identity, they talk in ways that avoid conflict so as to be safely social.

Recall Gloria sharing her teaching experience about taking a stance. She was vulnerable to face threats because she was putting her teaching out for group examination. To help her out, Lesley, the university facilitator with one kind of professional authority in the group, reframed her coaching of Gloria to refer to what we wanted the "kids" to do rather than what Gloria should have done. Ccil, with the authority of high professional and social status, also referred to the "kids" to save face for Gloria.

Right after Ceil hedged and awkwardly floundered for words to correct Gloria's misunderstanding, another high social status participant, Renee, a department chair, tried to help out. As observable in the transcript that follows, Renee also referred to the students instead of to Gloria.

Transcript 6.6

CEIL: Kids need to have a clear understa:nding of

Taking a specific stance↓

>I don't know

Help me with this<

RENEE: I I I think I'm going down the same road. But I'm not sure. I was wondering if I if I could. . . .

And I was wondering if, so many times we ask students

The alignment of Lesley, Ceil, and Renee moves to deflect any face threat to Gloria's teacher identity, which was so intertwined with how she wanted to be perceived socially in this group. It decreased the likelihood of further threats to Gloria's personal identity, which was closely tied to her teaching, and decreased the likelihood of Gloria opting out of the group.

Gloria's and the other group members' further discursive moves continued working together throughout the remainder of Gloria's explanation of her teaching. The result of all their face saving and power circulations was a social realignment of Gloria as a recognizably competent member. Because Gloria and the other members made it possible for her to save face, they made it possible for her to be a learner who could remain open to learning from her colleagues. And, because Gloria safely resumed the learner position, the rest of the group was positioned to learn with her. Otherwise, if Gloria had been positioned out of alignment, as deficient and incapable of learning, the group's dynamics would have been unaligned. Without everyone experiencing the conditions of self-efficacy, aligned purpose, identity recognition, personal and common understanding, shared assumptions, and meaningful choice, the group would have difficulty functioning as a learning community.

This dynamic applies for student learning communities as well. When one of their peers is called out in public by a teacher, students respond to the shift in power and social alignment. For example, Jolene's classroom community dynamics could have shifted had Jolene not been aware of the social nature of Rena and Ben's attention-getting antics. By siding with Ben, Jolene demonstrated one way to reposition Ben so everyone could quickly get back to learning. Had Jolene not aligned with Ben and, instead, reinforced Rena's *That's stupid*, and berated Ben's silly writing topic suggestion of *how the blue bear ate the lunch box*, she might have escalated the situation and disrupted the learning. Adolescents will most often take the student's side against the adult authority figure. With younger children, a similar dynamic can occur. Even those who aren't the target may often feel threatened by a teacher's powerful authority.

Also important to consider are the differences in the recognized social status among the students in the classroom or teachers in the group.

Status: The relative position or standing of persons in a social group.

Face threats and face saving are linked to the status of those involved. When the person making the threat has higher social status than the person being threatened, the effects are even more costly to that person's social prestige. When speakers with higher status make an effort to provide face-saving conditions for those with less status, as Ceil and the facilitator did for Gloria, or as Jolene did for Ben, the results are much more positive.

The power of teacher discourse is substantial. Teachers can speak in ways that reinforce unequal academic and social statuses of their students or of their colleagues (Cohen & Lotan, 1995).[14] Face threats and face saving are a way of understanding how communicating the status of those involved creates unequal treatment (Watts 1991).[15] The greater the speaker's social status, the more powerful the threat to the recipient. It's understandable why students and colleagues are silent or stop showing up.

Try It Out: Saving Face

Notice a time when you save face for a student. Try to recapture the moment. Who said what to whom with what effect? This type of question is considered classic among those who study classrooms as social communities.

The next time you find yourself in a difficult conversation in relation to your teaching, whether with a student or a colleague, ask yourself: Who said what to whom with what effect? What can you learn from the interaction?

Chapter 7

Building Knowledge

Why bother with all these complicated views of discourse, interaction, positioning, alignment, status, identity and self, worlds, interdiscursivity, power and face? Our answer is that these ways of understanding interaction help us understand how knowledge is constructed socially. If we understand the dynamics of constructing knowledge socially through language acts, we are better able to be intentional in building learning communities. We can also participate more productively in learning processes. In this section, we focus on building knowledge. We want to demonstrate how learning is a social process, and how teachers can be more intentional in the ways they go about helping students learn what teachers think they should know.

Recognizing Teaching Discourse

In a professional development workshop she was facilitating, Laura began by asking the teachers, "How many of you begin a lesson with 'Who can tell me or who remembers?'" Everybody's hands went up in recognition of a form of discourse spoken by many experienced teachers. Asking students to recall and represent knowledge from their previous lesson(s) is standard procedure for reinforcing previous learning and setting up new learning. The interaction is structured something like this:

Transcript 7.1

TEACHER: Who can tell me what you know about immigration?

STUDENT: (Raises hand)

TEACHER: Yes. Jane?

JANE: (Jane offers a partial answer)

TEACHER: Okay.

Who can add to what Jane has said?

A teacher will call on Jane, who will say something, and the teacher will say, "That's right." Maria will say something else, and the teacher will say, "Uh-uh" and "Who can add to that?" Sometimes she will call on another student before saying something like, "That's absolutely right," followed by a restatement of a point she wants to remind the class they learned.

In Laura's session, when she provided this explanation, all the teachers nodded in agreement. So Laura said:

> Well, think for a moment. How many of you have boys in your classrooms? And how many of you have children of poverty, English language learners, or African American students? Their discourse patterns may or may not be the same as yours. They may not be school congruent.
>
> We know, based on census data, that we have a White, female, middle-class teaching force and will have for the remainder of our careers. Children who speak a discourse other than a White, female, middle-class way of speaking have to work harder to engage in the conversation. So when you start out by asking who remembers, and quickly accept the answers of three students without elaborating, the child who's not used to that pattern may be lost before you ever get to your teaching point.

Usually when Laura says this, teachers say "Ah-ha" in recognition. Most teachers have been looking for a way of teaching they can rely upon for all their students. In this instance, one teacher took offense. She said, *Do you mean to say that by the time I get a child in eighth grade he has not learned teacher discourse?* Laura explained that most of these students spend a great deal of their time outside of class in other discourse patterns more familially, socially, or personally meaningful to them, and they have to work harder when they come into class. They have been working harder for a long time and, though physically present, are disengaged. As soon as they recognize this teacher talk, they turn off. It is often not a matter of *can* they, but rather do they *want* to engage. Laura wanted teachers to understand that their teacher inquiry discourse was unproductive if students did not respond as inquirers. What use is recalling content if students aren't interested in using it?

What can teachers do with and for students who respond this way? A teacher cannot learn all the discourses children use or are familiar with. However knowing *that* they use multiple discourses is a good start. It shifts understanding so that teachers realize that starting the same way each time—with teacher questions meant to recall prior knowledge or a previous lesson—is not necessarily a way into inquiry for all children or young people. So they need to reconstruct their practices to include all possibilities for genuine inquiry.

Asking Genuine Questions

By genuine inquiry, we mean that students are interested and engaged in wanting to know more. They ask their own questions, and these questions reflect their interest in understanding more. We assume that this condition is what teachers are aiming for when they construct a learning community. The classroom from which the next excerpt is taken is an anomaly in this particular high school. It is the only class required of all students, except PE, that is not tracked. Diagnosed with learning disabilities in second grade, Judy has spent most of her time in classes designated for the learning disabled. This is the first time she has encountered a class with a full range of student categories, including gifted and talented.

The pedagogy and curriculum for this intentionally de-tracked class were planned to make possible the participation of all the students. This excerpt, from a few weeks into the semester, is taken from a discussion that followed the viewing of an evening news video about immigration. The teacher's objectives were to get students talking together to share information and to see each other as resources. He was also preparing them to conduct independent research, culminating in a research paper. The teacher, Jack, began with genuine questions to prepare students to pursue inquiries on topics of their choosing. It is common for higher achieving students to offer interesting and research-worthy questions. Jack purposefully designed his lesson to elicit questions from all his students, so that those who often remain silent or mimic more assertive students' questions would authentically participate.

By this time in the semester, when Jack called for *genuine questions*, the class understood them as *questions you really want to know the answer to that anyone could ask and all would benefit from hearing.*

Genuine Questions: Sincere questions teachers or students want to pursue as opposed to questions the teacher asks to determine who knows the correct answer.

Judy speaks up for the first time in Jack's class, to ask her question. She wonders what happens to undocumented immigrants when they are discovered. The video the class has watched is a news report about the influx of undocumented immigrants coming across the border from Mexico. The video shows border guards patrolling desert roads and small groups of men, women, and children struggling to cross the sand. This school is in a part of California heavily populated by Mexican immigrant families, and a number of class members are Mexican or Mexican American, though Judy is Anglo-American.

Jack redirects Judy's question to Linda, a Mexican immigrant, who visits regularly with family in Mexico. Linda hopes to be the first in her family to graduate from high school. Earlier she had talked with concern about the new immigration bill passed by the voters calling for educators to turn in undocumented students.

Transcript 7.2

JUDY: OK. What about the immigrants? If they find you, and, like if you xxxx. If they find you on this side . . . and . . . and you're doing something illegal, or something, can they say go back? Can they put you like in a . . . what do they do? Can they put you in our jail? Or what do they do?

JACK: And you're not a United [States citizen] legal prisoner here, what do they say? Go back?

JUDY: If you commit a crime in this country?

JACK: That's a good question. That would be a good question [for further research]. I think they would . . . (to Linda) Do you know the answer? What would they do? They would try them for the crime in this country?

LINDA: Yeah. They do.

JACK: Yeah. If you've committed a crime. I have a friend who works in San Diego as a border patrolman, and a lot of people come here because you can make so much more money than you can over the border. So they come to the United States to work and find jobs. And a lot of times what he will do . . . they . . . it's almost like a game of tag because people will be coming and it's not like they are coming armed with guns and stuff, because most of them are not violent people. They are just "OK, you got me." And it almost sounds like a tag football game out there some nights.

        (Linda and students laugh)

        Because they have these scopes and the people get on the bus and they go back over the border and they just come back later on and try to . . .

LINDA: (Interjects) They come back and do it again.

Jack's interaction has taken two students of lesser social and academic status and given them more social and academic power.[16] He has positioned a special education student and a minority student as having something worthy of contributing to the group. When Judy asks her genuine question, and Jack responds, *That's a good question*, and answers, he has circulated the power to Judy. She is positioned, along with her question, as having worth, and put in the position of a learner. This act works toward establishing values and dispositions in the class: all genuine questions and student questioners are equally deserving of attention, all questions have equal status, and all students are resources. Judy's question provides an opportunity for new knowledge to be built. In this context, the question is every bit as important as a response in building knowledge. The question sets up a series of social interactions that build learning. Later, students designated gifted and talented asked different questions in different ways, and they were responded to differently. The way in which the teacher engaged with each student modeled and reinforced all students' contributions as opportunities for learning. In this way, the class experienced an inquiry approach in that their questions and responses contributed to the class's learning of the first steps in identifying a research question.

The information that Jack supplies in response to Judy's question and the manner in which he does so is of interest to everyone in the class.

Transcript 7.3

JACK: That's a good question. That would be a good question [for further research]. I think they would . . . (to Linda) Do you know the answer? What would they do? They would try them for the crime in this country?

By validating Judy's question and turning to Linda, whose personal experience may shed light on the question, and telling students about his friend who is a San Diego border patrolman, Jack brings his world, the world of his immigrant students, and the world of academia into alignment. His story also provides a model for how to socially present knowledge that could be face threatening for some people in the class. Jack is aware that a number of the students may be illegal immigrants or have immediate family members who are. He models an academic discourse that shows students how to take up potentially divisive material, presents it in a way that is not offensive, and leaves it open for further investigation. He avoids judgment, and discourages it among the students who, because they are from different social and cultural worlds, commonly make that move first.

After ten years of teaching in this school, Jack has a reputation as a well-liked teacher with a knack for telling stories. The students' response to Jack's move—laughter from Linda and the other Latino students—

signals that he has made a good discursive choice in this instance, which may be how he earned that reputation. He selected and shaped the information into a story. In doing so, in a way that students recognize as meaningful, he also created a model of what counts as knowledge and knowledge-building. Knowledge can be personal narratives from experience; experiential knowledge becomes valuable knowledge for the task at hand when it is presented in a way that can be heard by the others in the room; to be heard as educative, information requires attention to meaning and understanding, which are always both personal and social.

Jack was not aware that he was making these discursive moves. As an experienced teacher, he had learned over the years to carefully gauge his students and adjust his teaching accordingly. What we are trying to accomplish with this example is to provide a vocabulary for what teachers say and do that creates successful learning. We are challenging the notion of the *born gifted teacher*. By learning how to observe and analyze the ways in which teachers and students interact, the craft of teaching can be available to beginning teachers and developed more consciously and, we think, more effectively.

Now that we have presented this version of the interaction in Jack's classroom for one purpose, we want to reconsider it for another. We think it is time to be reminded that there is not one right interpretation of an interaction, but rather interpretations from different points of view. As a participant observer in Jack's classroom, Lesley brought extensive ethnographic data to her interpretation of this interaction, including interviewing the students involved as well as Jack. As you read the transcript you probably created a different reading and interpretation of what was happening, because you referred to contexts you have experienced to make sense of it. One of the applied linguists who reviewed an early manuscript of this book provided a counter-interpretation, which we think is a productive example of how a brief transcript can be read by someone who wasn't "living" in the classroom. This reading is critical of Jack's discursive moves as counterproductive and derogatory:

> An alternative interpretation could be that once Judy got her question out, Jack took over the construction of knowledge by telling his own story about his border patrol friend. We never hear from Judy again, so it isn't evident in the transcript that Jack gave her any academic power—and if we examine Jack's talk, he doesn't actually take up Judy's "genuine question" ("If you commit a crime in this country?"). Instead, he talks about the economic reasons why people come across the border and makes light of deportation activities using the metaphor of tag football. So, an alternative interpretation could be that Jack is not co-constructing knowledge but co-opting what gets talked about and doing so from his own, rather narrow perspective, and might actually be making light of a very serious human rights issue that may effect the lives of many of his students

and/or their friends and families. It may be that Linda's and the other students' laughter is not a sign of agreement, but evidence of a certain degree of discomfort with how the topic of illegal immigration is being trivialized by their teacher.

In addition, it might be that Jack, by deferring Judy's question to Linda, a Mexican immigrant, is positioning Linda as the "spokesperson" for illegal immigrants, a positioning she may very well resent. We really don't know how Linda feels about this positioning because all she says is, "Yeah. They do," and later, "They come back and do it again." So, it is hard to see in the transcript how Judy and Linda have gained social or academic power. Perhaps if we heard from Judy or Linda again later in the transcript we would be able to see how Jack's talk, as Lesley claims, "works toward establishing values and dispositions in the class: all genuine questions and student questioners are equally deserving of attention, all questions have equal status, and all students are resources" (p. 56). It is also unclear how Jack's talk "models an academic discourse" that "avoids judgment, and discourages it among students." This may very well be the case, but this interpretation is not evident in the transcript. So much of Lesley's interpretation comes from beyond/behind the transcript, from the rich ethnographic work in Jack's classroom.

Though this proposed interpretation is inaccurate in the sense that it is not borne out by what the students and teacher in the classroom that day said was happening, it can be imagined as a possibility because we have encountered discourse storylines like this one. The brevity of the utterances makes this storyline possible. No single transcript can provide all the contextual information possessed by a reader who was on site when an interaction happened. However, as we well know, even people in the room have their own interpretations depending on the frames they bring to the interaction. We make a point of reminding you of this situation not to discourage you from analyzing your own classroom talk. Rather, it serves as a reminder not to assume that your interpretation is the only one or the right one. We want it to be a useful one, in the sense that it opens up learning for your students and makes you a better teacher. How discouraging it would be if our self-analyses simply reinforced our inaccurate perceptions of our teaching.

Because of Lesley's insider knowledge of Jack's classroom, we could select the interaction to illustrate a consistency between how Jack acted and his beliefs that knowledge is socially constructed, that students learn with and from each other, and that all students bring valuable resources to the table. His utterances demonstrate that he can act upon his beliefs. In doing so he is more likely to create a classroom in which his beliefs become the social values, beliefs, and dispositions of the students. When teachers accept that knowledge is built through interaction in interdiscursive worlds, then all contributions have value because they set up strings of discourse that create new meaning for the hearers and speakers. They set up the interplay between personal learning and social learning. Recognizing and making use of the teacher and student worlds that come together in interaction allows us as teachers to take seriously the funds of knowledge that everyone brings to the curriculum.

Try It Out: Genuine Questions

This is a twofold assignment. First, pay attention to the questions asked in your classroom. Who does the asking? Are the questions "genuine"? Do questions go beyond checking to see if students can tell you what they know or learned? What proportion of questions do you ask? What proportion of questions do students ask? Are they questions about directions or requests for permission or genuine wonderings related to content?

Second, pay attention to which students ask questions. Are there some students who rarely ask a genuine question? Can you become aware of opportunities for marginalized students to contribute personal knowledge that may lead to greater social status?

Tape one class lesson. Play back and write down your questions. Write down student questions. What do you notice? What discursive options become visible to you?

Close Readings of Text

In Jack's example, we showed how the teacher provided knowledge in a way that considered the social dimensions of his classroom as well as its personal meaning for some of his students. The teacher shaped and presented the knowledge to serve social as well as academic purposes. With the next excerpt, we illustrate how the teacher takes a different discursive role during knowledge-building. We will unfold that role by asking you to observe what the students perform through their talk, before we show you the teacher's discursive moves. This excerpt comes from a discussion after a reading quiz about the class text *Beowulf*.

Beowulf: An Old English heroic epic poem dating to the early Middle Ages. In the poem, the hero Beowulf battles three opponents who are attacking Denmark. *Beowulf* is the only heroic epic poem to have survived from that era and is traditionally taught in high school English classrooms.

Now, if you are an elementary classroom teacher reading this account, do not skip this example. It is standard practice for teachers to discuss readings with students. How they go about it in ways that build knowledge is the focus of this example.

The discussants are eleventh graders in an English class **tracked** for "gifted and talented students."

Tracking: Sorting and separating students into classes by ability. Tracking is often found in high schools which can include Advanced Placement classes, high, average, and low ability classes as well as special education classes across a range of academic subjects. In most contexts, once a student is assigned to one track, it is difficult to move to a higher level of course work.

Though the curriculum is rigorous and the pace swift, the teacher allows any eleventh grader to enroll if she thinks she can keep up. As a result, half the students in this class have been in regular tracks since elementary school while the other half have been in gifted and talented classes or pull-out programs.

The transcript begins with Dave, the teacher, requesting student answers to the first quiz question: *So what was Unfrith's role?* Notice what gets said, by whom, and when. The purpose of your reading is to understand how the utterances, or speech acts, are performing in interaction.

Transcript 7.4

DAVE: All right, let's talk about some of these things. So what was Unfrith's role?

ANDREA: What was it?

Oh, about a guy who told the story about things that he planned.

JIM: [He kind of questions Beowulf Beowulf's

BOB: [Power

JIM: [Power. Power and bravery.

BOB: Yeah, but then Beowulf

MARK: It was also to show that uh people were jealous of Beowulf and and his power and he was questioning more Beowulf's wisdom not his power

BOB: Yeah. Yeah

MARK: Yeah

Notice that single utterances *restate, answer, finish, acknowledge, point to, interrupt, extend*, and *qualify*. Notice also that we can determine how each utterance performs by reading it in relation to the other utterances, especially the one(s) immediately before and after. For example, when read alone, Andrea's *What was it?* appears only to be a direct question. However, knowing that the teacher's question *So what was Unfrith's role?* precedes Andrea's *What was it?* we can conclude that Andrea's question performs as a restatement of the teacher's original question in this interaction.

Even though, as is most often the case in educational conversation, interactants do not speak in complete or grammatically correct standard English sentences, we can understand what is being said and performed. In this case, we can conclude that, taken all together, these interactive speech acts provide an original answer to the teacher's question. Andrea seems to restate part of Dave's question before answering. Jim provides an answer, and as he does Bob finishes his sentence, saying *Power* at the same time as Jim and adding *bravery*. Bob acknowledges Jim's addition and begins to make a point about Beowulf. He is interrupted by Mark, who provides an answer to the teacher's original question about Unfrith's role, which extends and qualifies what Bob and Jim have said. Another sense we can make of this quick series of interactions is that the four students readily answer the teacher's question *together*. They spontaneously construct a common answer with a number of interrelated points. Together they convey that Unfrith's role in the narrative was to tell a story about what was planned and to tell the story in a way that questioned Beowulf's power, bravery, and wisdom. Also, the students convey that Unfrith showed that people were jealous of Beowulf and of his power and questioned whether Beowulf was wise.

In this sequence we see power circulating among the four students so that with each turn each speaker experiences the power of his or her knowledge being the right piece at the right moment for what is expected. They each understand what the person before them has said and respond to it in a way that builds knowledge of use in the moment. That is, the students confirm for each other that what they are saying about Unfrith's role is an acceptable reading of the text because they each build on what the other one says. We can understand that power is circulating and that the knowledge is being built collectively without knowing anything about Beowulf and Unfrith. We simply need to read the discourse.

The next transcript is the second version of this reading segment. We have written it in a different form to highlight the speech acts as units of sound and meaning. Each new line beginning with a capital letter reflects a new start of talk after a pause. By representing the transcript this way, it visually separates the teacher's speech acts from the students', while also showing when they happen simultaneously. The first *Beowulf* transcript made it easier to see the roles of students' acts among themselves in constructing an answer. They appear to have talked this answer into existence without the teacher saying anything.

The students did carry on discussions without the teacher's input later in the year, but not at this point. The teacher was part of this interaction, and enacted a particular role. We removed the teacher's utterances in the first transcript so you would focus only on the students' interactions. In this next transcript, we reinstate the teacher's words, but separate them from the students', so as to get a different view of what was said, when, and by whom. The circulation of power now appears wider, and our view of alignment, positioning, and status changes. As you read the transcript, notice how in the interaction the teacher is positioned into his role. He is both the authority and not the authority in the interaction.

Transcript 7.5

TEACHER	STUDENT(S)
All right	
Let's	
Let's talk about some of these things	
So what was Unfrith's role?	
	ANDREA: What was it?
What was it?	
	ANDREA: Oh
	About a guy who told the story about things that he planned.
He stands against	
	JIM: (interrupts) He kind of questions
	Beowulf
	Beowulf's
	BOB: Power
	JIM: Power
He does	Power and bravery

He questions

That's right
Yes

And in fact Brecca won the swimming event, right?

But that's what Unfrith said.   BOB: Yeah but then Beowulf

                                       MARK: it was also to show

                                       That

                                       Uh

                                       People were jealous of Beowulf and
                                       his power

                                       And he was questioning more
                                       Beowulf's wisdom

Yes, though Brecca did say that uh   Not his power.
That Beowulf was defeated

I mean Unfrith said that Brecca beat
Beowulf.

                                       BOB: Yeah

                                       Yeah

But that's true

Your other points are excellent

Right

It makes him

Doesn't it make him more real?

                                       MARK: Yeah

When Dave begins by saying *Let's talk about some of these things*, and
then asks *So what was Unfrith's role?*, the students appear to think they
know what he expects by *talk*. They launch right into answering. Andrea
goes first, and when Dave begins to add to what she has said with *He
stands against*, he is interrupted by Jim. Jim asserts that Unfrith *kind of
questions* Beowulf's power. This move prevents power from circulating
back to the teacher and redirects it to Bob. Jim and Bob's alignment
reinforces their joint construction of an answer. They are not only

reinforcing each other's power as readers, but also their status as sources of knowledge in the classroom.

Before Jim finishes his final move, the teacher re-enters with a confirmation of their answer: *He does. He questions. That's right. Yes.* Dave is positioning himself in the role of final authority for what constitutes a correct answer. He also adds to the answer—*And in fact Brecca won the swimming event, right?* His *right?* is a request for a confirmation, which does not come. The students are silent. Dave steps into the silence to provide some evidence to argue for his point: *But that's what Unfrith said.* Dave is acting to get back into the conversation, reassume his authority, and provide more information. However, his information about Brecca has the effect of shifting attention away from the students' focus on Beowulf.

Bob acknowledges what the teacher has said without taking it up: *Yeah, but then Beowulf.* This *yeah, but* construction repositions the focus of the answer on Beowulf and in alignment with what has already been said by Jim, and provides the opportunity for Mark to align with Jim and Bob in the building of their line of reasoning.

So what has the teacher been doing here? While Mark was speaking, Dave attempted to shift the alignment so that it aligned with his answer's logic: *Yes, though Brecca did say.* . . . Dave used a *yes, though* construction to acknowledge the logic Jim, Bob, and Mark were building while opening up the possibility that it could be contested. Dave's move appears to be another attempt to circulate power back to himself while keeping the students' interest in continuing their line of thinking. As a more knowledgeable reader, he was offering new information from the text as evidence for their points—that is, Unfrith reported that Brecca beat Beowulf which shows he is not all-powerful.

Again, students didn't take up the teacher's information, and Dave stepped in, this time to confirm that their points are *true* and *excellent.* Bob was quick to confirm Dave's opinion of their work, and when Dave asked whether Unfrith's narrative made Beowulf seem more real, Mark didn't hesitate to agree. He and Jim and Bob have established that Unfrith's role in the legend was to bring into question Beowulf's power and wisdom. In other words, Unfrith was taking Beowulf down a peg or two from superhuman to human. Dave's final question and Mark's response serve to confirm that all the interactants have been engaged in constructing a similar line of reasoning about the character Unfrith's role in the story. Unfrith's narratives gave Beowulf human dimensions that made him *more real.*

Dave's final question models a *so what* closure for the reading. A common reading practice in this classroom, a *so what* is the reader's interpretation of the importance or significance of a reading. The *so what* in this case is the student understanding that Unfrith's role is to make

Beowulf appear more real or human. Through their close, collaborative reading they built a common reading, or meaning, for the text—that Unfrith's role is to make Beowulf seem more like a heroic man and less godly.

In this interaction, power has circulated during the construction of a reading of a character's role and of the reading's significance. The circulation profile is unique in how it flows among the students as well as among the teacher and students. Everyone who participated had an opportunity to experience power and status in the knowledge-building. In some respects the teacher and students remain aligned throughout. That is, the teacher remains the superior knower with the right to final judgment. In other respects, the students are empowered by the practice norms of the classroom to construct their own answer without joining the teacher's reasoning. They exercise power in the knowledge-building as well as receiving the affirmation of their teacher.

Conclusion to Part 1: Introduction to Discourse

We can now return to our original question: Why bother with all these complicated views of discourse? It is an important question and in the parts that follow we will provide answers having to do with building knowledge, difference, and testing and accountability. Jack's and Dave's interactions with their students preview the first of the three parts. These classroom interactions illustrate how the teaching and learning of subject matter is visibly performed through discourse. Though brief, the analyses of these excerpts gave us a way of seeing how subject matter becomes meaningful content as teachers and students engage with it. We can see content knowledge being interdiscursively built in an inquiry approach. Jack's students are learning how to ask and answer genuine questions for each other, on their way to learning other dimensions of research literacy. In Dave's classroom, students are building nuanced close readings of text, which provide the substance for the essays they will write. In both examples, whether the teacher or the students provide the knowledge, social interaction is key. The teachers and the students interact in ways they all find personally meaningful and socially powerful. Consequently, they remain engaged and open to opportunities for learning.

Try It Out: Interactions as Opportunities to Re-see Our Teaching

Before trying out these ideas in your own classrooms, let's try on some of the key constructs previously discussed. This transcript freeze-frames an interaction during a fourth grade grammar lesson. The teacher wrote several sentences on the chalk board and asked small groups of students to decide which parts of the sentences were the subjects and which parts were the predicates. Subjects were to be underlined once. Predicates were underlined twice, verbs circled. This transcript picks up when the teacher reviews the answers with the class. A student reports out from the first group.

Read through the transcript with the following questions in mind:

(1) What knowledge is being built?
(2) How are the students positioned as learners?

Transcript 7.6

STUDENT: The sentence that we're going to do is number 1.

"Actors in wagons traveled around the country."

Our subject is "actors in wagons."

And our verb was "traveling."

And our predicate was "around the country."

TEACHER: Okay. What's your predicate? Whoa.

What's your complete predicate?

STUDENTS: "Traveled around the country."

TEACHER: Thank you. "Traveled around the country."

But you picked up. What helped you to find your predicate?

You found your what? What did you put your circle around?

STUDENTS: "Traveled."

TEACHER: Which is your what?

STUDENTS: Verb.

TEACHER: Okay. So they found . . . What this group did . . .

They found the verb and they circled the verb.

When they found the verb I know that's the one to start my . . .

STUDENTS: Predicate.

TEACHER: And do not exclude your verb. Your verb is included in your predicate.

So you must have a line under the verb as well as everything else. Everybody got that?

Here is our thinking in regard to those questions.

What knowledge is being built?
In this interaction, knowledge of how the teacher expects students to do these sorts of grammar assignments is the primary knowledge being built. Although this was intended as a grammar lesson, it reads more as a confirmation of how to do the lesson than as an extension of students' knowledge about subjects, verbs, and predicates. To "see" this more clearly in the transcript, let us reread line by line to understand the interactions.

In lines 3–8, except for a minor misreading of "traveling" for "traveled," the student begins by providing a correct answer for the assignment. The teacher then has a number of choices for how she can respond to the student. After correcting the student's minor mistake, the teacher asks, *What helped you to find your predicate?* The student responds correctly, *Traveled*, which the teacher asks him to label as a verb. The student complies. Now the teacher restates for the class what the group did correctly.

Acknowledging the students' correct answers can be viewed as a positive teaching move. However, in lines 15 and 16, the teacher states, "They found the verb and they circled the verb," emphasizing the action of correct circling. She finishes the interaction by telling students to include the verb in the predicate by underlining the entire phrase.

A pivotal moment of choice occurred in lines 15 and 16. What if the emphasis was on the function of the verb in that sentence and other sentences, rather than on the circling procedure? Could students have learned something in that exchange that could be useful beyond the level of the assignment?

How are the students positioned as learners?
To think about this answer, once again, we reread the transcript. The student's first words are, "The sentence that we're going to do is number 1." This way of talking indicates the student knows what is expected in this lesson. Students are going to DO number 1. Students are positioned as reporters of what they have done for the assignment. As the interaction progresses, the teacher's responses to the students' reports continue to position them in this way. The teacher speaks mostly in directives, asking for a report. "What's your complete predicate?" "You found your what? What did you put your circle around?"

The issue is not that this is a "bad" lesson, but that this is a lesson about procedure. Unavoidably, teachers spend some portion of their time talking about procedures. However, transcripts that freeze-frame episodes that occur with frequency in our instruction can help us re-see what we are valuing when we enact curriculum.

Try It Out: Co-constructing Meaning

Once again, set up a camera in the back of your classroom. Try to capture a conversation when you and your students co-construct meaning. It could be a discussion of a book or a discussion in some other school context. Select an example where both teacher and students are collaboratively making meaning.

Now, create a transcript of the excerpt you want to study.

First, create the transcript in linear order of utterances by both you and your students.

Second, separate out your talk from your students' talk. Place the utterances side by side as in the example of *Beowulf*.

Third, analyze the talk.

What meaning are the students constructing? How do students build on one another's utterances?

How does your talk interact with that meaning?

Do you and your students share the same line of reasoning?

Part 2

Curriculum

Introduction

Learning subject matter is a primary goal of teaching, and making subject matter meaningful to our students is key to them wanting to engage and learn. As we observed in Jack's and Dave's classrooms, successive communal engagements with materials, ideas, and procedures allow the building and meaningful internalization of knowledge. We observed how Dave and his students built readings by interrelating different meanings of the text from their different worlds. Their individual utterances about what the text meant relied upon a history of exposure to discourses about interpreting literature. They each voiced these discourses so as to build a new, collaborative and agreed upon meaning.

We can learn from Dave and his students that to build knowledge, and to be changed in the process, requires time and social community. Time is necessary to build the relationships that allow for cooperation and the willingness to stay in the process even when it gets difficult. In Dave's case, he kept trying to insert his interpretation, and his students chose to politely position him out of their discussion. Perhaps they were not ready to hear his contribution, or perhaps they were too wrapped up in their own thinking. We cannot know. However, we can see that Dave's choices of how to respond indicate that he knew how to shift **alignment** so that students had room to play out their own knowledge-building. Power circulated within aligned interactions among text and talk—that is, interdiscursively.

When the social group purposefully aligns through multiple successive moments of negotiated meaning, individuals can experience powerful learning. A challenging and authentically rigorous and transformative curriculum depends on the build-up of trust and collaboration. If educators and students are to flourish as learners, they need to be aware of how they are **positioning** themselves and others. They should aim for social **alignment** and respect the personal **stake** they have in the way their **identities** are viewed.

To observe more directly how positioning, alignment, stake, and identity are constructed in the ways teachers talk with students, we compare two conversations taken from two eleventh grade English classrooms. Both teachers are interpreting their district's writing curriculum.

Chapter 8

Positioning, Alignment, Stake, and Identity I

Jolene and John

In this chapter, we revisit the interaction between Jolene and John from Jolene's English classroom which we used to illustrate how positioning and identity are created in interaction. This time, we add alignment and stake to observe what Jolene and John were constructing in that inter-action as curriculum and learning. We observe the construction of what counts as essay writing as Jolene confers with John about the penultimate draft of his paper. Their conversation took place near the end of the school year at Jolene's desk at the front of the classroom. Notice how Jolene's instruction positions John as a writer and positions his writing as not meeting the expectations of the curriculum. Jolene implores John to *think of a better way to say that* because he's *a better writer than that* (5), while John struggles to make sense of Jolene's comments and to resist her prescriptions for improvement.

Transcript 8.1

1. JOLENE: Ok, with the title of a book, you underline it and put it in italics, not quotes. Now I didn't fix it every time you did it because know when you fix this to go back and do that. What's this <u>right</u> <u>he:re</u>?

2. (3 second pause while she waits for John to answer. John silently reads.

3. JOLENE: <u>You.</u> <u>No personal pronouns.</u> Get 'em out, anywhere you find 'em. I found a couple, you may find some others. Awkward. (Jolene reads John's paper) "A good theme that can be used in book two, 'Flight,' of *Native Son*, is the concept of blindness." A <u>good theme</u>, how could you say that a little bit better?

4. JOHN: It was 2 a.m. when I wrote it.

5. JOLENE: Okay, well let's think of a better way to say that, 'cause you're a better writer than that. A <u>good theme</u>, come on . . .

6.   (A student hands Jolene a paper and waits at the desk)

7. JOHN: What's wrong with the concept of blindness?

8. JOLENE: (Jolene checks and returns the paper)

9. JOHN: What's wrong with the concept of blindness?=

10. JOLENE: =Nothing, it's not it's not the sentence, it's the way it's worded. (.7) The sentence is fine. The way it's worded isn't—a <u>good theme</u> that could be u::sed.=

11. JOHN: =Should I rearrange the words? (.6)

12. JOLENE: How about something like "A theme prevalent in book two of *Native Son.*" Do something like that=

13. JOHN: =If I knew what prev- alent means?=

14. JOLENE: =It means it's in there a lot. It's throughout the out the book. Okay, can you do that, can you switch it to something like that rather than saying a good theme that can be used? 'Cause a theme isn't something, it's prevalent, that's what you're saying, is you're talking about the theme of blindness here, you're not, you're not <u>using</u> the theme. The author uses the theme, you're not doing that.

15.   (Excised talk: Jolene quiets students.)

16. JOLENE: Show me in your conclusion paragraph where you restated your thesis (hands John the paper).

17.   (3 second pause)

18. JOHN: The thesis wa:s the first sentence up here.

19. JOLENE: Um, okay, that's not right, that's a problem.

20. JOHN: Why, was it supposed to say something else?

21. JOLENE: Yeah, actually, I don't (3.5) (She reads the peer reviewer's comments) Brad said it [the thesis] was this (points to a different sentence), and I also thought it was that. You know why, why would I think it was that?

22. JOHN: Because it was the ending sentence.

23. JOLENE: Right. I mean either one [sentence] works for your paper, so you want to put that here then, right? (writes on paper) Thesis goes here. So then it is restated, and then you're good. (hands paper to John) Alright? So fix those up, and give me a final draft on Wednesday.

24.   (John remains at desk)

25. JOLENE: Yeah, the thesis is the last sentence of the first paragraph=

26. JOHN: =It always is?

27. JOLENE: That's the way we do it here. (.5) At Merriman High. That's the way most of your English teachers here should be doing it. If they're not, I, I don't know what to tell you.

28. JOHN: In the conclusion, at the first=

29. JOLENE: =It can go anywhere in the conclusion as far as I'm concerned, as long as you restate it, Ok?

Jolene appears firmly in control of this interaction, a conversation that she begins by outlining problems she sees in John's paper. She focuses on his wording and its placement. John's efforts to save face are meek and earn him little status. At first he injects light humor, *It was 2 a.m. when I wrote it*, to which Jolene does not directly respond. Instead she identifies John as a writer who is better than this performance suggests, which may imply laziness or at least a lapse of attention related to the 2 a.m. writing time. Rather than directly challenging this imputation of his performance, John is concerned that the unifying concept of his essay has been challenged. He asks, *What's wrong with the concept of blindness?* Phrased as a mild challenge, Jolene meets it head on with *Nothing* and redirects her critique of the draft to its wording and away from its concept. John meets this critique with another veiled challenge—a concrete question, inhabited by exasperation with a touch of sarcasm, *Should I rearrange the words?* (11). Jolene takes over and shows John what she wants by rewriting his sentence, incorporating the word *prevalent*, with which

John is unfamiliar (12). John's comeback to Jolene's instruction to *Do something like that* is to mock his own ignorance and perhaps teachers' attempts to co-opt students' writing and make it more sophisticated than they feel it needs to be, *If I knew what prevalent means.*

As is often the case during individual conferences, the teacher needs to quiet class chatter. When she returns to the exchange, Jolene points out an additional problem—John's placement of his thesis in his first paragraph. Jolene tells him it should always be the last sentence. He meets this criticism with a weak *It always is?* Jolene invokes the authority of the school to retain the status of her knowledge: *That's the way we do it here. (.5) At Merriman High.* She rearranges John's opening paragraph by physically marking the changes on John's paper and pronouncing the text *good* (23).

Though John asserts himself, power does not appear to circulate in this interaction. Jolene remains in the power position throughout as she constructs John's identity as a writer, his writing knowledge, the curriculum he is to learn, and his next steps as the writer of this essay. When Jolene says, *That's the way most of your English teachers here should be doing it. If they're not, I, I don't know what to tell you* (27), she makes a particular kind of complex and powerful teaching move to establish her position with John in relation to his past experience with other teachers. She adds authority to her role as teacher by acknowledging that his other teachers may not have been doing what they should have been. Perhaps this move allows John to save face. His prior teachers, not he, may be to blame for his not knowing this way of writing. However, the move complicates instruction because, of course, there *is* such a thing as a delayed thesis. It is possible John knew there were other (sometimes more effective) ways to present a thesis.

Throughout this interchange Jolene believes she is productively assessing John's learning needs and concretely responding in ways that he can use to improve his writing. She has the authority of the school curriculum behind her. Each time she speaks, Jolene invokes authoritative status as the knowledgeable teacher evaluator and positions John as the less knowledgeable student.

What knowledge of writing to improve his performance is John gaining from this interaction? If all of his writing knowledge is gained through interchanges with a critical reader, and for this semester that is this teacher, then what knowledge will he learn? Is this the same as the curriculum that Jolene believes she is teaching? Furthermore, how will John understand writing and being a writer? We know from our observations that John is a polite, soft spoken, serious inquirer, who thinks deeply about issues raised in the literature the class is reading. Often during class discussions he asked challenging questions or presented intellectually interesting and off-beat points, which the class respected. He placed ideas and being a responsible citizen of the class ahead of earning a good grade.

In this conversation about his essay, John's manner in the class is evident. He listens carefully to his teacher's evaluative comments, attempts to understand what she is asking of him, and offers mild protest. In the face of Jolene's insistent directives, he inquires to clarify what she means. He seeks information about the quality of his ideas, but acquiesces to his teacher's focal interest—how they should be encoded. In this interaction, his ideas are not acknowledged in a way that lends him power, or addressed in a way that builds more than superficial knowledge. How does this interaction shape him as a writer and as a student of writing?

Chapter 9

Positioning, Alignment, Stake, and Identity 2

Stan and His Class

The following excerpt from Stan's 11th grade English classroom provides a contrasting view of how writing curriculum and students' writing are shaped along with their identities as writers. Prior to this interaction, Stan had one of the students read aloud a passage from Ernest Hemingway's *A Farewell to Arms*, which the class was reading. The passage Stan chose is a long paragraph, consisting of multiple clauses connected by the word *and*, containing no terminal punctuation marks. Stan comments on the length of the sentence, and a student asserts that his previous English teachers would not have allowed students to write that kind of sentence. Other students agree, and Stan takes the opportunity to teach what he thinks is important about writing.

Transcript 9.1

1. JANE:	U::hm last year Mr. S would like say that was really wrong.
2. MIKE:	Yeah, I know!
3. JANE:	He would, like, mark it off and stuff.
4. MIKE:	<u>Ye::ah</u>
5. STAN:	Why would he, why would he mark it off?
6. JANE:	I don't kn:o:w. If it was more than a li:ne long, he'd off the pages
7. JERRY:	He didn't know "And"=
8.	=(Class laughs)

9. JANE: He'd put a big X (she makes slashing movements
                with her right arm)

10. STAN: He didn't like you to connect your words with
                "and"?

11. MIKE: Yeah but he liked his papers lengthy, though.
                That's what I didn't get.

12. STAN: You mean he didn't like long sentences?

13. MIKE: He didn't like long sentences, but he liked lengthy
                papers.

14. STAN: O::: hh. (0.4) Well (0.6) Mr. Hemingway <u>DOES</u> it.

15.   (3 or 4 students laugh)

16. STAN: (0.8) So:o I guess you could do it to:o (0.3) if
                you've got a reason for it not just to have a real
                long sentence, but there's got to be a reason
                behind it. By the way, what are some other things
                you hear about what you should do in your writ-
                ing? (Goes to chalkboard) Let's just take a quick
                break. What have your teachers told you before
                about writing?

17.   (Students call out rules for writing, and Stan lists
                them on the chalkboard)

                No "ands" or "buts" or "because" to start a
                sentence
                5 paragraphs
                No "I" or "you"
                Thesis is last sentence of the 1st paragraph
                One topic sentence for each paragraph
                No contractions

18. STAN: Well, we could probably go on and on, but you
                know what the simple fact is? (Crosses out the list
                with a giant X) [That none of these are rules

19. BOY: [All of these are rules

20. GIRL: Oh, they're just <u>their</u> own rules, too.

21.	(Stan lifts his arms to shoulder height to perform an upper body shrug at the girl)
22. MARY:	Oh, wow.
23. ROBERT:	They're rules on the [state standardized test].
24.	(7 students laugh)
25. STAN:	(.5) There are no hard, fast rules there. Sometimes it's good to do that, sometimes maybe it's not (1.5) [Ok?
26. MONICA:	[I like this class=
27. JANINE:	=[Me too=
28. MARY:	=[I know=
29.	(5 students laugh)
30. STAN:	What we're going to do is we're going to be writing things that, doesn't necessarily, where you don't have to put all this stuff in there. Ok? We'll talk a little bit more about it. I just wanted to introduce you to how I see writing. And sometimes good writers don't use that stuff up there, they don't follow those things. Maybe sometimes they do, it depends on what you're writing. If you're writing a love letter to, to your boyfriend or girlfriend, is it going to be in five paragraphs?
30. FOUR STUDENTS:	[No. [Uh-uh
31. STAN:	No, probably not, probably not. Ok. Good. we'll get back to some of these rules or non-rules . . .

In this segment of classroom conversation, we see Stan positioning the reading curriculum (*A Farewell to Arms*) as writing curriculum in a particular way. He is also positioning students' prior knowledge of writing in an attempt to position them as writers in his classroom. We can say that Jolene was similarly engaged in positioning a literary text as writing curriculum in an attempt to position John as a writer. Both Stan and

Jolene align with their English teacher colleagues, but with different interests and different views of writing curriculum at stake.

By saying, *Mr. Hemingway DOES it. So, I guess you could do it too* (14, 16), Stan draws a distinction between the rules for writing illustrated by a renowned professional writer, and those of the students' other English teachers. Jane contests, saying her previous teacher would not allow students to write that way. She underscores this by saying he would *off the pages* (6), and mark them with a big X (9), while making a dramatic X gesture with her arms. The rules Jane learned in previous English classes resonate deeply. Other students agree. They, too, received either real "X's" on their writing or marks with similarly deep resonance, and those experiences frame how they approach writing in Stan's class.

By saying, *Well, Mr. Hemingway DOES it*, Stan positions himself with "real writers" and positions students to question their former writing instruction. In the rest of the interchange, Stan asserts a view of writing for everyday life in the students' world, in which they emulate "real writers" and choose the rules they will follow. He projects writing as liberating rather than restrictive, and context-bound rather than arbitrary. This is a message his students are willing to hear. Years of not measuring up to the rules for writing their teachers laid down predispose them to prefer an approach which contests the rules.

In his next gesture, Stan dramatically positions himself as the antithesis of the rule-making teacher. In doing so he separates himself from all their other teachers, and hopes to separate the students from their frustrating experiences with writing. Stan appropriates the X that served as such a powerful symbol for Jane and the other students, theatrically crosses out the rules on the board, and symbolically nullifies the rules the students have learned, stating *the simple fact is that none of these are rules* (18).

Student responses to Stan's claim are mixed. One girl interprets Stan's point as these are simply the teachers' own rules, not *the* rules of writing, which Stan's dramatic shrug confirms. Mary expresses this new awareness with *Oh, wow*. However, other students remain wary of this new approach. It is a student who introduces the serpent in the Eden of no rules writing. *They're rules on the [state standardized test]* (23). He is referring to the test all the students know they will have to take that year, which teachers are supposed to be preparing them for. That many of the students laugh at Robert's serious comment indicates their agreement with Robert's point and their appreciation that he "got" Stan. Their unpleasant reminder of reality is ameliorated when the authority figure is bested by one of their own. For most of them, this will be the third time they have taken the test, and they assume it will probably be the third time they score poorly. Another big X on their writing record. This turn in the class conversation is not where Stan wanted to go. He finds his footing and reasserts his position. Even on the [state standardized test] there are *no hard, fast rules* (25).

Stan's response was to ignore the allusion to the test and return to his argument that *sometimes good writers don't use that stuff up there* (30), *it depends on what you're writing*. Stan asked students to think about possible writing situations and to use what they know about what is and is not appropriate in those situations to determine which "rules" to follow. He positioned them as knowledgeable in ways that promote good writing. Some of them liked this identity, and some remained skeptical.

What knowledge of writing to improve their performance are Stan's students learning from this interaction? If, throughout the semester, Stan's responses to their writing are similar, what knowledge will they accumulate? Is this knowledge of writing the same as what Stan believes he is teaching? How will Stan's students identify as writers in school, and for their next English class? Our observations of the remainder of the semester revealed that students continued to struggle with writing, especially with development of ideas and concrete text-based problems of organization, grammar, and punctuation. Yet, as in Jolene's classroom, they remained present and engaged. Stan continued to encourage them to see school-based writing as no different from what "real writers" do.

In Jolene's and Stan's interactions we could observe two different contexts of writing instruction. Both teachers were interested in establishing what counted as essay writing. Though brief, and certainly not representative of all their writing curricula, these comparative interactions highlight noteworthy differences. In neither interaction does power circulate. Jolene claims the authority for herself and Stan gives it to the students. Like you, we want these acts to be complemented by many more interactions in which power is circulated while meaning is negotiated. Fortunately, in these classrooms they were.

Nevertheless, these interactions serve as illustrations of stultified knowledge-building because Jolene and Stan did not recognize and take the opportunities that were afforded. In neither of these interactions were the writing identities students were expressing acknowledged, nor the stake they had in learning. Jolene did not provide John with an opening to present his concerns about the point he wanted to make with his essay, and Stan did not address students' concerns about testing and other English teachers. They were out of alignment. Neither teacher aligned with students in ways that might build social alignment respectful of individual stake. By claiming all authority for herself, it would be unlikely that Jolene's students would have the confidence to respond critically to each other's drafts. Stan's students would most likely have had similar trouble if authority remained solely in literary authors. His students already identified as unsuccessful writers, and deducing how to write school essays from Hemingway's style is a challenge even for the most confident of student writers.

Chapter 10

Minimizing Face Threats While Challenging Practice

Twelve math and social studies teachers representing grades 4–8 met for the fourth session of a two-year professional learning sequence. Their district had committed funds for staff development to increase student learning by building teacher leadership in content area literacy. This goal involved building a common language across grade levels from elementary through middle school.

The series was collaboratively envisioned and planned by lead teachers, their assistant superintendent, and Laura, their county literacy consultant. We knew that this would be a difficult conversation because it threatened teachers' identities and their notions of competency. Such conversations made them vulnerable to bald face threats, in which the speaker makes no attempt to minimize a face threat. To place teachers in a position of respect for one another, Laura borrowed the National Writing Project model of teachers teaching teachers. In year one, the middle school teachers would plan and facilitate content literacy practices for their middle and elementary school colleagues. The second year, elementary teachers would plan and facilitate literacy practices that would be applicable for their middle school counterparts. A number of questions framed the assessment measures planned for the workshops. The planners wanted to know whether the teachers would teach what they learned from each other. As well, they wondered whether they could construct a less face-threatening community that would permit a circulation of power, in which people were willing to accept critique and self-assess.

The first session focused on metacognitive tools such as Think Alouds to help teachers model disciplinary thinking for their students. Session two addressed understanding comprehension strategies, text structure, and text format. After each session, teachers were expected to try out new approaches with the support and encouragement of a colleague also involved in the staff development series. Initially, we stayed with comparatively safe curricula conversations, which we hoped would build community and trust. It was not until the third session that we increased the rigor of the curriculum, increasing the likelihood of face-threatening acts. We asked teachers to report their classroom successes to the group for discussion. To address this potentially socially destructive situation in which teacher identity was at stake, we initially turned to predesigned protocols.

The Protocol

A protocol frames the purpose for and manner in which teachers share their classroom experiences, modifications, and student work. It structures and times conversations so as to visibly manage how teachers share and question one another's practice or student performance. The protocol directs conversation by assigning turn-taking, limiting the duration people can speak, and directing each speaker's focus and purpose. Protocols limit the focus and constrain content as well, which is why they should not be over-relied upon. However, in this instance Laura found a ready-made protocol appropriate for the workshop situation: the *Success Analysis Protocol* (SAP). This protocol matched the conditions the workshop leaders wanted to create. It would keep the teachers' first exposure to a protocol as supportive and collegial as possible by focusing teachers on what they regarded as their successes, on what worked in their teaching and why. Focusing on the positive would help cushion possible discomfort caused by making teaching visible to colleagues for examination. In discourse analysis terms, the structured conversation of the SAP would make it easier for teachers to remain in alignment with one another and limit face-threatening acts.

The protocol Laura used comes from Teachers' College Press at www.tcpress.com. Numerous protocols are available on this site to be downloaded and modified as needed.

Success Analysis Protocol

Purpose: To engage colleagues in collaborative analysis of cases from practice in order to understand the circumstances and actions that make them successful ones, then to apply this understanding to future practice.

Details: Twelve to thirty participants in small groups of three to six. Chart paper. Notepads for participants. One to two hours.

Steps:
1. *Preparing a case.* Participants prepare to describe one area where they are finding success or making progress in practice. May be done in advance.

2. *Sharing.* In small groups, first person shares his or her case of successful practice. Others take notes.

3. *Analysis and discussion.* Group reflects on the success. Participants offer insights into what specifically contributed to success. Presenter is encouraged to participate and can be prodded through questioning.

4. *Repeating the pattern.* Repeat steps 2 and 3 for each member of the group.

5. *Compilation.* Groups compile a list of specific successful behaviors and underlying principles that seem characteristic of the cases presented.

6. *Reporting out.* If there are multiple small groups, the groups report.

7. *Discussion.* Surprises, commonalities, underlying principles.

8. *Debriefing.* Applications to other areas of our own work? Uses with students?

(www.tcpress.com)

The first time the protocol was followed, the conversations were a bit stilted. It was difficult for teachers to imagine using the format in team or staff meetings. However, with use, the protocol process became less artificial and more conducive to meaningful teaching and learning conversations.

During the fourth session of year one the facilitators and Laura planned to use a protocol other than the SAP. The protocol they selected is called a *Collaborative Assessment Conference* or CAC. They aimed to build on that first experience of sharing teacher practice. This time they probed deeper and more critically into student work and teacher practice. For this session, teachers were asked to bring recent assignments that reflected intellectually challenging tasks. The teachers as well as the workshop leaders wanted to consider whether they were teaching what they thought they were. They intended to assess the intellectual rigor in their assignments in relation to state standards and to what scholars in the disciplines hold up as sophisticated examples of student learning. The odds of face threats were high because in a CAC participants are asked to affirm their colleagues' teaching and student work and also to question and suggest alternatives. Teachers' identities were at stake, so Laura and

Richard, the teacher facilitator, designed each aspect of the all-day workshop to reduce risk.

In the morning the CAC framed teachers' sharing of student work. Teachers were more familiar with sharing their practice and knew from their positive first encounter with the SAP that their colleagues would act in ways that minimized face threats. So, conversations flowed more easily this time. The focus in the CAC was on student work and not on teacher practice. Everyone knew that looking at student work and not at teacher practice would minimize face-threatening acts. The goals were to notice what students were having difficulty learning and to design next lessons that would support further understanding. Note the three layers of observation: describing, raising questions, and speculating.

Collaborative Assessment Conference

Purpose: To sharpen teachers' perceptual skills by looking deeply at a single student's work; to encourage a balance in perception; to help teachers see how they can act individually and collectively on what they learn in order to benefit their students.

Details: About 45 to 90 minutes. Five to thirty people. Student work—one piece rich in detail or several pieces from the same student (e.g., a portfolio). Copies for participants or post around room.

Steps:
1. *Presenting.* Teacher presents student's work with minimal context. Participants examine the work, making notes.

2. *Describing.* Group members describe what they see in the work. No judgments.

3. *Raising questions.* "What questions does this work raise for you?" Participants respond. Presenting teacher listens and makes notes, but does not respond.

4. *Speculating.* "What do you think this student is working on?" Participants respond. Presenting teacher listens and makes notes, but does not respond. The facilitator presses for evidence.

5. *Responding.* Presenting teacher responds as he or she chooses: to offer additional context; to share thoughts about the student work; to respond to any other questions regarding the student, the context, the assignment, and so forth.

---

6. *Reflecting and discussing.* Open discussion for reflection on the experience. Participants may share what they found particularly helpful or difficult while participating in the activity, or ideas about use of the protocol in their own work with colleagues and/or students.

In describing, no judgments may be made. In raising questions, the presenting teacher is protected by not having to respond directly to the questions. In addition, the questions only address what the student has produced. The third layer of observation involves speculation regarding what the student was working on or trying to do. Note that the facilitator's role is to "press for evidence." This grounds the comments in the student work in front of the group, removing the teacher as the subject of discussion. In discourse analysis, a bald face threat is a direct insult. It weighs heavily against someone's face, challenging a sense of self or identity. In a CAC, though the stakes are higher than usual in a teacher-to-teachers group share, by not permitting the questioner to ask about the teaching or the presenting teacher to respond, the teacher is protected from inviting or receiving bald face threats.

The CAC took up the entire fourth morning. The protocol was useful as a vehicle for sharing practice and student work so as to maintain social alignment and production of understanding and knowledge. Also, the conversation was more extensive, fluid, and relaxed than it had been with the SAP. Teachers knew they would be protected. However, along with these gains came some limitations. Maintaining safe group equilibrium became the reigning norm. Most teachers honored the student work and couched any questions or speculations in the most positive of terms. Questions and speculations tended to be more superficial than probing. Laura realized the teachers would benefit from developing new ways to think and talk about student work, and believed they were ready to do so because of the politeness norms they had established.

Raising the Bar for Student Assignments/Tasks

As the protocol was not sufficient to move teachers beyond norms of face-saving collegiality, to more challenging discussions of teacher work, Laura and the teacher facilitator decided to abandon protocols. They planned an afternoon in which to work with the group in building their own common language to productively talk about teacher tasks. Familiar with the Authentic Academic Achievement (AAA) work of Fred Newmann, Walter Secada, and Gary Wehlage (1995),[17] they chose to begin with AAA as one way of looking at and analyzing teacher assignments that generate student work. The risk of face threats would be increased by shifting the attention from student work to teacher assignments, and teachers might be uncomfortable in front of their peers if their assignments did not live up to high standards. Therefore, Laura and the facilitator built in face-saving safeguards. Had they not done so, they most likely would have closed down receptiveness to challenging established practice.

Participants were asked to think of a lesson they had assigned recently that involved higher order thinking and jot it down for their own personal reflection later in the day. Next, they were invited to read and discuss the standards for authentic pedagogy (Newmann, Marks, & Gamoran 1996).[18] The standards offer a more complex way of thinking about assignments in terms of disciplinary rigor. The seven standards include: organization of information, consideration of alternatives, disciplinary content, disciplinary process, elaborated communication, problem connected to the world beyond the classroom, and an audience beyond the classroom. When looking at assignments through the lens of AAA standards, no one task or assignment is expected to address all of the standards at high levels. Rather, application of the standards to the activity tasks gives teachers a means of assessing academic rigor and relevance in order to view the strengths and limitations of particular assignments as well as offering possibilities for deepening subsequent tasks.

Setting aside their higher order thinking lessons, at first the teachers practiced analyzing and critiquing lessons written by others outside the group, so as to understand the standards and how to use them before they critiqued each other's assignments. First, they read and discussed the meaning of the AAA standards. To apply them, they looked at several tasks or assignments from the New Standards work (www.NCEE.org), a collection of student performances linked to high standards for academic achievement. In like content areas, teachers read only the tasks that accompanied examples of student performances. Then, in small groups, they scored a task high, average, or low for each AAA standard. Their discussion revealed their lack of understanding of the first standard: organization of information.

Standard 1: Organization of Information

The task asks students to organize, synthesize, interpret, explain, or evaluate complex information in addressing a concept, problem, or issue.

Consider the extent to which the task asks the student to organize, interpret, evaluate, or synthesize complex information, rather than to retrieve or to reproduce isolated fragments of knowledge or to repeatedly apply previously learned algorithms and procedures.

> To score high, the task should call for interpretation of nuances of a topic that go deeper than surface exposure of familiarity.

Laura realized the teachers needed to build their understanding of the standard before they could proceed to productively assess their own tasks. Until now, she had been scaffolding activities to manage the dance of alignment and face threat. It seemed that at this moment in her planning, attention to social equilibrium through positioning, alignment, stake, and identity was less important than additional scaffolding. She wanted to challenge what she viewed as a thin conception of the standard so that she could later have teachers apply this more rigorous standard to their own assignments. She had to do so without sacrificing the social community or teachers tuning her out.

For help, Laura turned to her teacher facilitator, Richard, and asked if she could use his assignment. Laura hoped that his status in the group would mitigate any threats to his face that might arise. He graciously agreed. His willingness to serve as guinea-pig indicated some degree of confidence in the quality of his assignment.

Laura began by asking the group to read Richard's assignment and score it according to all of the standards. Once again, group consensus placed the task high on organization of information, confirming for Laura the group's misconception about the meaning of the first standard. With Richard's permission, the assignment is reproduced on pages 88 and 89.

The group appeared to confuse assignments that required students to follow complex directions with assignments that required students to engage in cognitively complex disciplinary reading and writing. I hoped the teachers would see that their colleague's example provided complex directions for lower order retrieval and reproduction of material. Little complex thought related to the subject matter was expected of students. There was little depth of intellectual engagement. Instead, students were asked to manage literal meanings of text by evaluating and moving chunks of text into specific slots to complete the assignment. Information was seen as an exportable given, rather than as interpreted meaning that took into account management of ideas, perspectives, and evidence. Interactions like the following led Laura to that conclusion:

> "The task requires a high degree of organization," insisted Kathleen.
> "And what makes you say that?" Laura wonders aloud.
> "Look at how organized the student has to be to complete this assignment. He has to organize his pages exactly to specifications. Maps here, information here. Title just so."

Canadian Native American Tribe Book Project

You and your group will be making one or two pages in our book. These pages will be included in a class book about the tribes of early Canada. Your pages will include these things:

- Title of your page including the name of your tribe.
- A map showing where in Canada your tribe lived before Europeans came.
- Describe the Culture of the tribe.
  - ✓ Food
  - ✓ Clothes
  - ✓ Homes
  - ✓ Recreation; games, fun things to do
  - ✓ Weapons
  - ✓ Transportation
  - ✓ Language
  - ✓ Tools
  - ✓ Religion
  - ✓ Interactions with other tribes, how did they get along with other tribes (wars, friends, etc.)
- What happened to them when Europeans came? What was the impact of European expansion on your tribe? How do you think the native people felt when the Europeans came to Canada?
- You will present your findings and your pages to the class and the whole class will present your book at "Back to School Night."
- Think about an experience you may have had where someone was treated badly simply because of how they looked or because they were different. On a separate sheet of paper, write a paragraph or two about why people mistreat others and how the mistreated person must have felt.

Your 1st page should look like this. If you have more than one typed page, you will glue it on the back of your construction paper.

Sheet of construction paper

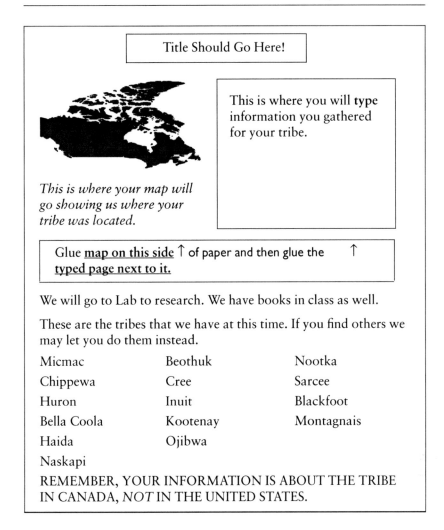

Title Should Go Here!

This is where you will **type** information you gathered for your tribe.

This is where your map will go showing us where your tribe was located.

Glue **map on this side** ↑ of paper and then glue the   ↑ **typed page next to it.**

We will go to Lab to research. We have books in class as well.

These are the tribes that we have at this time. If you find others we may let you do them instead.

Micmac	Beothuk	Nootka
Chippewa	Cree	Sarcee
Huron	Inuit	Blackfoot
Bella Coola	Kootenay	Montagnais
Haida	Ojibwa	
Naskapi		

REMEMBER, YOUR INFORMATION IS ABOUT THE TRIBE IN CANADA, *NOT* IN THE UNITED STATES.

To which Laura replied, "Is following directions the same as synthesizing or interpreting complex information about a concept or issue?"

Silence . . .

When she was unable to help the teachers distinguish between complex directions and assignments that require complex thinking and organization of ideas, Laura asked the group if they could analyze the assignment line by line to ask *what is being privileged here*. As she read each line aloud, she asked the group to stop her when she came to a line that required deep disciplinary content knowledge or higher order thinking. Of the two pages that comprised the assignment, the only bullet point that asked for interpretation of events beyond reproduction was:

What happened to them when Europeans came? What was the impact of European expansion on your tribe? How do you think the native people felt when the Europeans came to Canada?

Another paragraph in the assignment that asked students to identify with someone who was mistreated only tangentially connected to disciplinary content:

> Think about an experience you may have had where someone was treated badly simply because of how they looked or because they were different. On a separate sheet of paper write a paragraph or two about why people mistreat others and how the mistreated person must have felt.

The remainder of the assignment required reproduction of information lifted as is from the originating text or consisted of requirements that Laura termed "compliance requirements." Once each line was separated out and the task was analyzed for types of thinking, it became clear that most of this assignment asked students to follow directions. Students who know how to "do school" will earn high grades but may learn very little. The task privileged teacher authority, and limited student buy-in. The task structure narrowed the possibility of power circulation and of complex learning developing. The participation structure of the task did not encourage the shifting alignment of authority over possible meanings, which builds complex thinking.

When we revisited the task example from the New Standards work, the difference was evident. Teachers could see that they had read *organization* as organizing the material students were reading. The Turner essay sample task asked students to organize ideas. They were to read an original text in a way that interpreted and evaluated the ideas that the author expressed in comparison to the information they were learning in class. This called for selecting pertinent information from different texts (interdiscursivity) and synthesizing that information to create their own evaluative position. To do that they had to consider what Turner meant as well as organize their own selected and synthesized information as evidence for their point of view about what he said. This is quite a different expectation for intellectual rigor, and one that would have been completely missed in the other assignment.

The Turner Task

Evaluate Turner's frontier hypothesis and compare his theory of the westward movement in America with what you are learning in

> class about the actual events. Discuss ways in which Turner was both right and wrong, and whether or not his hypothesis was an accurate one.

The "aha's" were palpable. Clearly, Richard, the brave teacher co-facilitator who put himself at such risk for face threats, was crushed. The tension in the room was uncomfortable. Laura decided it would not be a good idea to return to the original assignments and reflect. Frankly, she was simply hoping she had not destroyed all the goodwill built over the previous sessions.

As happens in the classroom as well as in professional workshops, no amount of planning can anticipate moments of imminent face threats because of the learning challenge. They are inevitable. The dilemma is that without potential face threats, learning is less likely. Face threats are not in and of themselves bad or oppressive. They can become so when we do not prepare for them or repair them afterwards. In this case, Laura could have publicly thanked her co-facilitator for courageously contributing to everyone's learning. Without his willingness, the workshop goal could not have been fully realized. However, at the time, words failed the group, including Laura.

As the session ended for the day, teachers MaryBeth and Michelle loudly announced they were getting together over the summer to rewrite all their assignments. Richard acknowledged publicly that he had never looked at his tasks that way and planned to do a major overhaul. Laura remembered to breathe. The established community and good graces of the group allowed this to be a powerful learning experience. They never could have attempted such an "in your face" activity without first building trust and collaboration.

Similar to Laura, Dave, in the classroom discussion of *Beowulf* from Part 1, was responding in-the-moment, on-the-fly, to what students said during a group discussion. Like Laura, he learned what the students understood and responded to it. Also similar to Laura's group, he and the class had established social norms for what could be said and how it could be said during discussion by the time this interaction occurred. In addition, both discussions were about the group's reading of a text. In Dave's discussion, the students' responses led him to believe they could effectively interpret the meaning of a character in the text. In Laura's discussion, she discerned that the teachers could not interpret the meaning of the standard effectively, even though it made sense to all of them. Whereas the students' interpretation would allow the class to continue with a reading of "Beowulf" the teacher considered profitable, the teachers' interpretation of the standard limited their ability to increase the intellectual rigor of their curriculum.

Laura chose to use Richard's assignment as a text for further discussion.

As we learned from this example, not reading the text beforehand can have drastic, potentially destructive, consequences. Dave used similar strategies in his classroom throughout the term, asking his class to respond to a student's work. In interviews, those students asserted they found the practice helpful in improving their reading and writing, and not embarrassing, because of the way it was handled and because everyone did it. That does not suggest, however, that such practices went well every time Dave taught. Nor do we suggest that Laura's professional development community was face-threat-free. Taking face-threatening risks is necessary if curriculum is to be enacted so that learning occurs. From this perspective, teachers' and facilitators' effectiveness can be assessed by their strategic and responsive management of face threats so that all the members of a group learn worthwhile curriculum with and from each other.

Conclusion

To summarize, curriculum, no matter how well planned, is realized through the interactions that occur in social situations, whether in classrooms or professional learning sites. The lived curriculum in classrooms and professional workshops is what is constructed at the intersection of identity, social relationship, and subject matter knowledge. Curriculum is more than what is written on the page. It is also how what is on the page is brought to life through interactions during which power and status are at stake and continuously negotiated. Alignment, as managed through positioning, face, and interdiscursivity is a central consideration during these negotiations. When considering curriculum and instruction, with these constructs in mind, teachers are always asking themselves: *Are we teaching what we think we are teaching? How can we construct contexts that are less face threatening than others and permit power to circulate so that learners are willing to accept critique, self-assess, and build new knowledge? When we notice face threats or lack of rigor, how do we respond?*

As Jolene's, Stan's, and Richard's work has illustrated, freeze-framing rich interactions to reflect on the spoken and written discourse can make apparent curriculum teachers had not intended. Through discourse analysis they can interrogate their assumptions about what they count as teaching. Teachers can understand that learning does not occur as a direct relationship between what the teacher says and what occurs. Rather, learning is a social product from within and across everyday teacher and student talk. It is a constant negotiation of power, status, and identity. By looking closely at instances of interaction, teachers may come to see that to think they know what is occurring in their classrooms without close analysis is shaky business.

Without examination, our language can undermine the very objectives we work so hard to achieve. Through examination, we are better able to create alignment between our intentions and our teaching practices. In Jolene's case, her intentions appeared to be to improve John's essay writing. She had carefully considered what she believed was not working properly in his draft. Whether or not we agree with her writing instruction curriculum, we still recognize her fulfillment of her teaching responsibility to evaluate student work. Students need to know how they can improve their performance. Through analysis of her discourse, we were able to see the way she wielded her authority, but with such limited information we cannot know the effect of that authority. We cannot know if John got what he needed in order to grow as a writer. We would have to examine many more classroom interactions involving John over the course of the semester, and question John as well as assess his writing. We would want to know what curricula knowledge could be learned within the identities and social relationship under construction between the two and the rest of the class.

In Stan's case, he challenged traditional departmental authority. He drew his authority from literary writers such as Hemingway. He wanted his students to decide the rules of writing for themselves, based on the rhetorical demands of each writing situation. If lived curriculum is taught and learned in the intersection of identity, social relationship, and subject matter knowledge, to learn whether Stan's approach worked would similarly require looking at interactions throughout the semester. We know from conducting an extensive study of Stan's classroom that his approach worked well for some students, but less well for those who had long-established insecurities about their ability to read and write. They had heightened concerns about other teachers' evaluative criteria and about test scores.

In these two cases of lived curriculum, we could observe the issue of power and authority, and where curricula rules governing right ways of writing resided. Did they reside in the teacher, the department, the students, or literary authors? We meant to illustrate that they reside in all of these sites, but not as static entities. What counts as correct writing comes alive when performed or acknowledged through talk or activity by someone who experiences authority in a position of power. To conceive of power as something someone or some group *has* is not productive when considering teaching and learning. By their nature, teaching and learning are social and situated. Power is always moving interdiscursively. Even Jolene moved power around through her utterances. It was in her department's curriculum, in her authority as the teacher, and in Brad, the peer reviewer's comments. The ways she moved power served to align and reinforce her own powerful authority; but, at any moment, John or she could have said something to realign where the power was located. John did not speak from a position of power, nor did Jolene utter an opportunity for him to assume a powerful position. If power is the probability that someone will be able to carry out his or her will though there may be resistance, then John did not experience any of it. It may be that John is one of those students who is willing to do what he is asked by an all-powerful authority figure. However, we assume, based on motivation research, that most students are more willing to participate when they assume it is probable that they will exercise their will at some point in the learning process. Most students go along with the teacher as the powerful authority, but they expect to exercise their own power as part of a reciprocal relationship in their learning. There need to be sufficient occasions when students experience the power of exercising their will. Some literacy scholars recommend giving students choices, a direction taken by Stan. Others recommend students develop their own topics and rubrics. What one chooses should depend on the context and circumstances. However, a constant across all contexts is that power should circulate between teachers and students, while the degree and intensity will suit the circumstances.

In Richard's case, when asked he gave up his status and power to further the learning of the group. Laura accepted that power and the authority for analyzing his assignment on behalf of the group. Richard's sacrifice was worthwhile because the teachers' learning was intense and successful. In Jolene's and Stan's cases, blame and exoneration were key elements of the interactions. Blaming was used to exonerate and so save face and status. Jolene obliquely blamed John's former teachers—not present to lose face—so she could exonerate John and give him an opportunity to save face. *That's the way we do it here. At Merriman High. That's the way most of your English teachers here should be doing it. If they're not, I, I don't know what to tell you.* With this offer of exoneration Jolene provided John with a reason for why he could not know the right rules for essay writing. This shift in alignment moves Jolene into social relationship with John, which acts as a counterbalance for when earlier Jolene dismissed his identity as a thoughtful writer. This exoneration of John's underperformance could make him more open to the knowledge she imparted.

In Richard's case, blame and exoneration were not part of the interaction. The series of mediated experiences with a variety of protocols over time built confidence that efforts would be made to minimize bald face threats. In combination with strong norms of collegiality, the teachers did not turn to blame in order to exonerate themselves. The responsibility for the lack of intellectual rigor of their assignments was not placed upon their students' lack of ability, their department's lack of leadership, their students' parents, or pressures of standardized testing. The participants remained silent as they absorbed the realization that the responsibility was theirs, and it was up to them to make the necessary changes.

This is a best case scenario. In retrospect, we can analyze the conditions that resulted in this ending. However, we are well aware that there is no recipe for guaranteeing these results. If transformative learning is to have a chance of occurring, then teachers and administrators must recognize the imperative for sustained learning communities. Without ongoing relationships built upon successive interactions that allow power to circulate, face to be saved, alignment to be recovered, and identities as competent educators to flourish, professional learning that makes a difference in student learning will be hard to come by.

Part 3

Difference

Introduction

Single interactions can have profound effects on a classroom's social atmosphere or a student's participation. However, they fly by so quickly that we note only those that are extra-ordinary, when it is the accumulation of the innocuous ones that we should be attending to. Social relationship- and related knowledge-building mostly occur over the course of many fairly innocuous and unnoticed daily exchanges. For example, after the first month of a new semester, we could say that each class has evolved a unique identity with its own culture and ambience. Through hundreds of daily interactions, mostly unobserved by the students and teacher, common understandings of what is appropriate, who can and will engage and when, and what constitutes rewarded knowledge have been established.

To alter less successful, and to reinforce effective, classroom patterns of teaching and learning, it makes sense to look at what was said and done to construct them. As it is impossible to reflect on everything that is said, one needs a strategy for deciding where to focus. To determine a focus, we suggest beginning by noting interactions that display an issue a teacher is most interested in understanding. In Part 3, we will demonstrate how, once a focus has been selected, one might apply the discursive tools presented in Parts 1 and 2. Working with longer periods of classroom interaction, we make use of what we know about classroom teaching and discourse to look at *difference*, a classroom issue that continues to be of interest to teachers and teacher educators. To understand difference, and how to deal with it productively, we have decided to focus on two interactions in two classrooms, which we have already introduced. Keep in mind that if these were your classrooms you would have much more information about the students, the environment, and the actions that preceded each interaction. Lesley was in both classrooms when these events occurred and stayed on for weeks. However, rather than provide much more information (which you could find in Rex, 2006)[19] we will tell you only what we think is necessary to productively exercise the discourse analysis tools we have provided.

We know that students whose faces look like ours are not necessarily from our worlds, and we cannot assume they share our values and dispositions toward education. Neither are the worlds of students who look and speak differently from us necessarily different from our worlds. Given this complication, how can we productively conceive of difference? We suggest the best stance is to assume that students and their teachers are uniquely diverse, and that teachers differ in unique ways from their colleagues. This means that observing uniqueness should extend beyond standard differences common in schooling, such as race, ethnicity, class, gender, culture, and nationality.

Neuro-cognitive scholars such as Sydney Lamb (2000) explain that new research findings throw a special light on the links between language, culture, and thought. Lamb explains that this research elaborates on Whorf's hypothesis "that we cannot talk at all except by subscribing to the organization and classification of data which the agreement [of a speech community] decrees."[20] Lamb argues that people have different thought systems even within the same speech community or language-culture system. These neuro-cognitive thought systems produce "seeing," and different systems hard-wired into the brain explain why different people with fully functioning optical systems can see the same optical field differently. What is observed as diversity and similarity depends on what the observer's neuro-cognitive system translates as seeing. Included in this hard-wired system are an observer's values or preferences for what is seen, which result in unique observations and summary judgments of what is observed. Just as people within the same speech communities can see, understand, and value differently, so too can people within the same social and ethnic cultures. Diversity, it turns out, is much more complicated than the language categories commonly used to describe people—including the categories used by teachers, colleagues, and students to label patterns of human behavior (Agar, 1994).[21]

Everyone categorizes, which is defined cognitively as organizing and naming a category of information. As all people must, educators need to continually categorize to manage the large amounts of physical, emotional, and cognitive information they are receiving. Teachers' decisions about what to say and do next hinge upon what they observe their students are doing or saying during a lesson and how they name it. Teachers observe whether students are paying attention, understanding, being creative, or wasting time. Such categorizations of students' practices can determine whether pedagogy is responsive to students' performances. If a teacher categorizes a student's actions as "off task" when the student considers her actions part of her learning process, then it is likely they will clash.

One or two of these clashes over the course of a semester are unlikely to be a problem. But if this lack of alignment occurs with regularity, so that the teacher continually names the student's actions off task, it is highly unlikely that meaningful teaching and learning will occur with that student. Categorization of students' actions in cases such as this one becomes problematic for student learning when it occurs repeatedly and becomes a shortcut for understanding what is occurring. The student's actions, and by extension the student, are essentialized and assessed. The actions are off task and so the teacher identifies the student as inattentive.

Avoiding unproductive categorizing, while building productive categorizing, is key in keeping students engaged and learning. However, this move requires considerable attention and work. Neural structures are in place and new ones need to be laid. It is easier and more expedient for teachers to implement the categorical descriptors they have already acquired to understand what they observe in their classrooms. It requires effort and practice to develop new categories; therefore, teachers can easily fall into repetitive observational patterns from which it is difficult to find a way out. Nevertheless, because learning occurs interactively between teachers and students, such attention must be paid. To create and reinforce patterns of productive interactions or to change unproductive patterns involves recognizing one's own patterns of pedagogical interaction.

In this part, we focus on how teachers can analyze their discourse to identify unproductive categorization of their students' talk and behavior. We tighten the focus even further so as to walk readers through micro-analyses of difference based on race. Our illustrative analyses are meant to meaningfully complicate and unpack the two most common categories of race—Black and White. Teachers who can examine their discourse with students and colleagues to observe the role of unobserved and unintended racial essentializing and their outcomes have the opportunity to be more vigilant in their discursive practices.

In the two chapters that follow, we will illustrate types of complications that can occur among teachers and students of common and different races. We represent these complications as issues of social and academic identity in three separate cases, anchored by three separate transcripts. In Chapter 11, a single case depicts interactions among speakers of the same race. Difference seems to be getting in the way of the teacher's and students' purposes. A clash amongst the interactants puts a momentary glitch in what can be taught and learned and may negatively affect the social dynamics between those involved. In Chapter 12, two cases of interactions among speakers of different races illustrate how teachers and students can successfully resolve a clash before it becomes a problem. In each transcript, the teachers and students have different, conflicting ways of construing the problem that has created the clash. We illustrate how the teacher and students discursively negotiate these problems so that they are resolved for this situation and the lesson can continue. We conclude Chapter 12 by considering how we can usefully think about issues of race in relation to these illustrations.

Chapter 11

Clashes and Intersections of Teachers' and Students' Different Worlds

Case 1: Within Race

Challenging Assumptions of Sameness

With Marita's permission, we will look at another instructive interaction from her class. In the transcript below, all of the participants, including Marita, are African American. We have chosen this interaction to challenge assumptions of sameness; that is, a frequent assumption is that if participants are all White or all Black, they share ways of seeing and valuing common to their race, including common worlds with consistent norms for identities and ways of relating. This particular transcript demonstrates the limitations of this monolithic view of race. The transcript illustrates how race is complicated by issues of social status and identity, and how those issues interrelate to create and disrupt various alignments among participants. These shifting alignments are the daily social activity in classrooms that either furthers or inhibits learning.

The primary interactants are the teacher, Marita, and two of her African American male students, Byron and Jacob. The boys were good friends and identified themselves as "rappers," a style of speech they often exercised in the classroom, and that Marita encouraged. Switching in and out of African American Vernacular English (AAVE) and standard English, Marita spoke to students in an easygoing, conversational, yet maternal style.

During most class activity, students were talkative and socially engaged, lapsing in and out of playful verbal banter with each other and the teacher. Students called out their preferences as well as their answers. Marita let interchanges run their course, stepping in only if she believed an inappropriate boundary had been crossed.

In the following excerpt from a paragraph-writing activity in the fourth month of school, we observe Marita stepping in when Byron crosses a boundary and calls his friend Jacob's answer *stupid*. The episode occurs after Marita has asked the class to think up a concluding sentence to the first four sentences of a paragraph on the board they have collaborated in writing.

Transcript 11.1

1. MARITA: Okay. So, now you have another topic sentence, Jacob . . . And then you could tie in all of these together in one conclusion sentence. Let's go ahead and do that now since we've gotten this far (.) Could someone please think about it just for one minute. Once you have it in your head just raise your hand and share with the class.

(5 second pause)

2.   (Jacob raises his hand)

3. MARITA: Jacob.

4. JACOB: Let's see. As a result Alice's Alice illig I mean, dang=

5. MARITA: =go ahead

6. BYRON: [Patience. Take your time.

7. JACOB: [Alice's issues (.1) overcame her life.

8. BYRON: I thought she said figure it out and then say something.

9. JACOB: Playa, I don't think, Playa. I just freestyle.

10. BYRON: She said that because so there wouldn't be no dumb stuff said.

        [So think.

11. JACOB: [I just freestyle. Excuse me.

12. BYRON: I said what you said was stupid.

13. (Class laughs)

14. MARITA: No! No! Byron! Byron! Stop putting people down. Don't do that. That's not cool.

15. BYRON: I'm not trying to be cool. [I'm just trying to figure it out.

16. PATRICK: [Byron that's stupido.

17. (Loud class laughter)

18. BYRON: I'm being myself. [I'm just trying to be cool with people.

19. MARITA: [Don't. Don't. Don't put people down.
              Don't do that.

20. BYRON: What's the big deal? [How you gonna live?

21. PATRICK: [Tu el stupido   [Tu el stupido. (.5)
              [Tu el stupido.

22. MARITA: [Go ahead. Go ahead. Jacob. Jacob. Continue with what
              you were doing before you were so rudely interrupted.

23. JACOB: before before I was interrupted by this character over there.
              As a result Alice has uhm Alice damn man Alice's issues
              has=

24. GIRL: =you said taken over her life=

25. JACOB: =has taken over her life.

Jacob volunteered to give the concluding sentence. By waiting and raising his hand, he responded to the teacher's request to think for a minute
and signal readiness with his hand. However, he had only performed half
of her directions. He had not thought of a concluding sentence that he
was ready to share with the class. Byron responded supportively the
first time his friend stumbled over his words. But on the second try,
he concluded that Jacob had not followed directions and told him as
much: *I thought she said figure it out and then say something* (8).

Byron was playing for public status. Jacob's response to Byron, whom
he referred to in rapper vernacular as *playa*, was to claim that he was just
freestyling (9). Jacob was referring to the spontaneous rapping that the
two boys engaged in often, in and outside of class. This move identified
the boys as social partners who were aligned by their engagement in
social rap discourse.

Byron's response to Jacob sided with the teacher's school instructional
discourse rather than with the playful rap way of talking his friend
claimed as most relevant at this moment. Byron aligned with Marita and
spoke for the value of the school discourse, justifying why thinking up a
sentence before saying it was a better move than freestyling one: *so there
wouldn't be no dumb stuff said* (10). When Jacob exhorted, *I just freestyle* (11), as Byron said, *So think* (10), we see the clash between these two
positions. This clash led Byron to increase the intensity of the put-down

with a direct insult, *I said what you said was stupid*, at which point the class laughed (13).

For Marita it was all right to invoke rap discourses as long as student academic identities were not threatened. Marita read Byron's insult as crossing the boundary of social play and told him to *Stop putting people down. Don't do that. That's not cool* (14). Marita drew the line at insults aimed at a student's instructional performance. Byron attempted to justify himself when the class laughed at Patrick's remarks.

As happened occasionally, student academic performance was subverted, even though a student and the teacher attempted to reinforce academic learning. When Marita stepped in, Byron abandoned his alignment with the teacher's position and defended himself against public humiliation. He told Marita that he was not trying to *be cool*: *I'm being myself. I'm just trying to be cool with people.* In using this second application of "being cool" Byron placed himself outside the social game and in the school-rewarded discourse of individual responsibility for one's classmate, friend, or brother. He was just trying to be a good guy by supporting the teacher and helping his friend be a better student.

Jacob was doing what Byron accused him of—that is, he replaced the teacher's academic discourse with the social discourse of rap and all its attendant values. That Byron, himself a playa, challenged his friend's activation of rapper discourse by using the very attributes of the discourse to do so illustrates the complications of the moment. Byron invoked the social discourse appropriate for the situation to retain his social alignment with his friend. He also turned the form against itself. He used the form to disrupt the genre—or at least the values and dispositions it evokes—and align himself with his teacher and the academic enterprise. From this perspective, Byron's *How you gonna live?* is a plea made to contest Jacob's implied claim of future economic success through continuing as a playa and living the life. Byron's utterance aligns him with Marita and positions him as someone who can rap and be a social playa but who has chosen to do school.

In this case, the teacher and students engaged in common ways of speaking English. Through their language, they were negotiating identity and social relationships. Byron aligned with the teacher to continue learning how to write the paragraph, establishing himself as a committed learner. Byron publicly positioned Jacob in a way that socially threatened his student identity (lines 8, 10, and 12).

Transcript 11.2

   8. BYRON: I thought she said figure it out and then say something.

   9. JACOB: Playa, I don't think, Playa. I just freestyle.

10. BYRON: She said that because so there wouldn't be no dumb stuff
              said.

              [So think.

11. JACOB: [I just freestyle. Excuse me.

12. BYRON: I said what you said was stupid.

In self-defense and to save face, Jacob invoked a playa identity to regain
his status with his peers. At stake for Marita was her desire to inspire her
students to more consistent and meaningful academic engagement and
improved academic performance. She assumed an authoritative identity
when she said, *Go ahead. Go ahead. Jacob. Jacob. Continue with what
you were doing before you were so rudely interrupted.* Jacob responds to
her authority and reassumes his student identity. Marita has made it
possible for him to shift identities from a social to an academic alignment,
which the girl reinforces by reminding him of what he had said (lines
23–25). Note how Jacob expertly makes this shift so as to maintain
social alignment with the class and with Byron. He takes up Marita's
discourse—*. . . before I was interrupted . . .*—and refers to Byron as *this
character over there.*

Transcript 11.3

23. JACOB: before before I was interrupted by this character over there.
              As a result Alice has uhm Alice damn man Alice's issues has=

24. GIRL: =you said taken over her life=

25. JACOB: =has taken over her life.

Though the boys veered in and out of academic conversation, Marita
managed to return the class and both boys to the lesson. Marita may
or may not have been aware at the time that she was creating space
for her students to negotiate multiple identities without losing sight of
her teaching plan. With this transcript, Byron reminds us of his complicated stake in the interaction. Marita and Byron's interaction reminds
us to consider whether and how students can have competing stakes
in school discourses and in roles, and related identities, that are
antithetical.

  Few of Marita's interactions with the boys throughout the term
resembled this one. Most exhibited a much greater alignment in regard to
identity and role, but also in regard to meaningful purpose and content.
In other representations of the classroom in which this interaction

occurred, Lesley (Rex, 2003, 2006; Rex & Nelson, 2004)[22] used ethnographically collected data to represent other aspects of Marita's interactions with students and their outcomes for learning. These interactions illustrate additional ways of observing what categorization alignment and misalignment can produce.

Classrooms are characterized by interactions in which all the members (teachers and students) exhibit and recognize a common language for identifying class membership and the identity(ies) and role(s) of each member.[23] Each productive learning environment is characterized by an accrual of interactions in which the members acknowledge, utilize, and reinforce social identities that are positively meaningful to everyone involved.

There's Room for Differing Interpretations

Lesley has used the Marita, Byron, and Jacob transcript often with teachers so they can complicate their understandings of their classrooms and students. On one occasion during a presentation, she asked the assembled educators what this interchange allowed them to see. The purpose of the workshop was to demonstrate the benefits of looking at classroom talk to better understand issues of difference involving race. One of the teachers immediately raised her hand. The White, middle-aged female participant responded that it was obvious that this class was out of control and the teacher, Marita, needed to do something about it.

This teacher's view of the event in Marita's classroom is not uncommon. If Byron and Jacob had talked this way in the conference attendee's class, we might assume that she would have reacted differently. Or perhaps she would have established initial ground rules to prevent this type of interaction from happening. She might have enforced a "Don't speak out of turn" rule. We have no way of knowing if that style of interaction would have been a better approach for this teacher. However, what we do know is that we cannot simply discount Marita's response as ineffectual or applaud it as successful. It is never as simple as control or lack of control. By becoming aware of the complex negotiations students work through to adopt academic identities, we can consider how to act as teachers within those negotiations. Considering differences in race and social purpose complicates these negotiations even further. We suggest that going beyond control and participating in discursive identity- and relationship-building will result in more productive student engagement, especially for students raced differently from their teacher.

Marita and her students would say that they shared a common race. Yet, their interaction illustrates that complications in academic identity and social identities occur within race in classrooms. Differences within race are complicated by issues of class, nationality, immigration, culture, as well as age and gender. We will not address those here. Instead we want to make the point that successful negotiation of students' academic identity is a within-race as well as a cross-race challenge among students and teachers, and that discourse analysis will help teachers make decisions about what to say when these challenges present themselves in their classrooms.

We suggest that to productively view classroom interaction across these complicated differences means to ask: How can teachers create discursive spaces in which students' non-school-congruent identities can interact with situated academic identities—without the students or the teacher feeling threatened, or that their purposes have been derailed? How can teachers interact in these conversations to apprentice students into academic roles that satisfy both the teacher and student? How can teachers recognize these occasions as productive for building not only identity and social relationship, but also academic knowledge? If teachers can learn to observe subtle shifts in alignments, then they can make use of this observational skill.

Chapter 12

Clashes and Intersections of Teachers' and Students' Different Worlds

Case 2: Across Race

Challenging Assumptions of Difference

We return to Stan's classroom again, this time to illustrate across race discursive negotiation of identity. This second transcript illustrates how, once again, race is complicated by issues of social status and identity, and how those issues interrelate to create and disrupt various alignments between Stan and his student. In this case, more subtle shifts in positions and alignments allow an academically challenged student to remain in the discursive academic space without rejecting it. The interaction takes place in the hallway outside Stan's classroom. Of his twenty-three students, seventeen are African American, five are Arab American, and one has recently arrived from Cameroon. Stan is a middle-aged White male, and Sonandra, his female eleventh grade student, self-identifies as Black and African American.

It is the third day of the new semester and Stan has been going over a few rules for what is and isn't appropriate to do. Shortly after he explains why telling another student to "shut up" is inappropriate, Sonandra breaks that rule. At that point, Stan asks her to go out in the hall. She resists, but leaves, while the straight-faced class watches in silence.

Sonandra had been late to class that day, and had given Stan what school members call physical "attitude" when he inquired about the reason. This means she had rolled her eyes, turned away, and ostentatiously taken her seat. Later, she challenged Stan's rule about making up work with continuing "attitude," in her tone and physical posturing, which again Stan had overlooked. However, Stan could not overlook her "shut up." After completing explanations of the class rules and the class contract, Stan went into the hall to talk with Sonandra. Their conversation reveals the two coming to know each other as well as the stake they each have in their self-interests. When people reconstruct versions of events in their conversations, those stories they tell of "what happened" always create a version of events that reflects and protects their self-interests. In this case, Stan and Sonandra clash over their versions of what happened.

We can see how they position to protect the stake each has in an identity and purpose in the classroom.

We have divided the interchange into three pieces of transcript. Each section represents a different "problem" that the two discuss. Throughout their exchange they allude to what the other said. Also, in each interaction, what is being negotiated, how the negotiation plays out, and the consequences differ. Issues of status, authority, and power are at stake as Stan and Sonandra reposition themselves and each other by realigning where they stand. Through politeness moves, they manage to repair Sonandra's identity. In the first part of the interchange, their roles and relationship are quite different from those they assumed in the classroom where Stan had insistently asserted his authority. In the hall he is more of a reassuring inquirer, and Sonandra no longer gives attitude. Instead, she assumes the meek manner of a repentant child.

Transcript 12.1

1. STAN: Okay, what's the problem?

2. SONANDRA: What do you mean what's the problem? What's the problem?

3. STAN: Is there a problem?

4. SONANDRA: No.

5. STAN: Okay, Okay. Do you know why I sent you out in the hall?

6. SONANDRA: Uh-huh.

7. STAN: Okay=

8. SONANDRA: =I'm sorry.

During this first part of the conversation, Sonandra offers an unsolicited apology for eating candy (8). In the second part of their conversation, Sonandra asserts that she did not remember telling Brock to shut up, but apologizes again nevertheless, acknowledging Stan's authority and the authority of his rule. Then Stan tells Sonandra the two reasons he sent her into the hall, which she claims not to know. He identifies a second problem—her *bad mix* (17) dynamics with Brock, which contributed to her *acting up a little bit* (15). Stan infers that the two of them were engaged in flirtatious behavior. This time Sonandra's tone changes. No longer acquiescent, she sounds unconcerned as she dismisses the incident as not a problem. By saying they did not have classes together, she indicates that the two are not in a relationship and so this is simply a one-time minor infraction. This time, Stan acquiesces to Sonandra in letting her version of the problem stand. He then introduces a third problem when he says, *I want you to know I see what's going on* (21). Once again, Sonandra's tone and position change in response.

Transcript 12.2

9. STAN: For two reasons=

10. SONANDRA: =The candy.

11. STAN: And the "shut up."

12. SONANDRA: The "shut up"?

13. STAN: You told Brock to shut up. It might have been a playful way, but you did.

14. SONANDRA: Oh, I don't remember. I'm sorry.

15. STAN: Okay. (.5) Now. I have the feeling that there's a problem with Brock, because you were very quiet before he came in, and then you started acting up a little bit. I will separate you guys, because it looks like=

16. SONANDRA: =it's not a problem=

17. STAN: =it looks like you two together is, at least for, for order in the class, it's a bad mix.

18. SONANDRA: No it's not=

19. STAN: =Okay, I'll give it a [shot

20. SONANDRA: [We don't have any classes together=

21. STAN: =Okay. Well, okay. (1.0) But, you know, I want you to know I see what's going on. (.4) The comments you made Monday, to Francine, I didn't think were appropriate=

While Stan acknowledged Sonandra's playfulness in saying *shut up* flirtatiously to Brock (13), he took a different approach in addressing the third, more serious, rule violation. The previous class session, shy Francine from Cameroon had been persuaded to talk about missing her good life in Africa, where the people were friendly and took care of each other. In a mocking tone consistent with social talk common among students, Sonandra had responded, *Ahhh, we're not friendly to you.* Six African American students laughed at this. Then, Sonandra followed with, *We don't take care of each other*, which elicited more laughter. In the hall, Stan tells Sonandra that he does not regard her comments as appropriate, which alludes back to his class rules about not being disrespectful of classmates. Sonandra has no memory of being disrespectful. She remembers liking Francine's accent and acts wounded and incensed by Stan's accusation. She recalls treating Francine *like we was her family* (28), and just wanting to know how she felt, not meaning anything by her comments. When Sonandra adds *I mean, I would like to go there* (30), she appears to justify her connection to Africa, her respect for Francine's origins, and her genuine interest in questioning her.

Transcript 12.3

21. STAN: =Okay. Well, okay. (1.0) But, you know, I want you to know I see what's going on. (.4) The comments you made Monday, to Francine, I didn't think were appropriate=

22. SONANDRA: =Who's Francine?

23. STAN: The girl from Africa.

24. SONANDRA: What did I say?

25. STAN: Well, I think there was

26. SONANDRA: I said I liked her accent. That's what we talked about, her accent. I said I liked her accent.

27. STAN: But she also said that it was different there because, because everybody was friendly and she said=

28. SONANDRA: =No, I just wanted, I wanted to know how she felt, like we was her family. That was just a question. I wasn't saying nothing toward it.

29. STAN: If I misunderstood, I'm sorry. I apologize.

30. SONANDRA: Good, because I didn't mean anything by it, I was

just asking her a question. I mean I would like to go there, so.

31. STAN: Okay. Are we all set to come back in?

32. SONANDRA: Uh-huh.

33. STAN: Okay, there's no hard feelings on my part. Okay? But, you have the zero. Hang in there. Everybody's on a little five minute break right now. I passed out four other sheets, okay, you're going to have to read them yourself, and there's a contract in there that you sign, and that I sign, okay. I'm going to collect that at the end of class.

34. SONANDRA: Alright.

35. STAN: Okay. (Both return to the classroom)

Whereas Sonandra had been compliantly apologetic about her first "inappropriate" infraction and had gone head to head with Stan in an even contest on the second, with the third accusation she reverses the alignment and positions Stan's problem (and, therefore, Stan) as "inappropriate." Immediately, Stan acknowledges that he may have misunderstood and he apologizes, and she accepts his apology. Stan declares that he harbors no hard feelings, but Sonandra provides no insights into how she is feeling about the interaction. However, we know, as did Stan, that Sonandra's engagement with Brock, through the acceptance of his candy and their put-down banter, can be read as common gendered social flirtation among the African American students in this high school.

When we look at how Sonandra positioned herself in her first two exchanges with the authority figure, she appears to have appeased him so as to get out of trouble. However, in her third exchange Sonandra no longer appeased Stan; rather, she artfully took him on. She made a move that trumped Stan's authority. By alluding to Francine as "family," Sonandra's response aligned her with Francine as co-members of the Black family, and positioned Stan as an outsider who did not understand their world. Stan acquiesced to the position and acknowledged that he may have misunderstood, implying that he agreed that he lacked knowledge of her racial world, and therefore misunderstood Sonandra's purpose and stake.

What's at Stake?

All of this positioning occurred as the two negotiated how to perceive "the problem." The way Sonandra defended her accountability demonstrated the identity and social relation she was performing. She acknowledged what Stan identified as the first problem with candy, apparently not concerned that she was perceived by the teacher as eating in class. She denied his second vague claim that she was flirting, refusing any accountability, denying a problem, asserting this was not a relationship but rather typical casual social talk. She had some stake in the teacher not viewing her behavior as linked to Brock or to a continuing problem, or in not wanting to be reassigned to a seat away from the group of boys.

Sonandra forcefully refused Stan's interpretation of her interchange with Francine as the problem he described. Her discourse also expressed her interest in developing relationships with her African American classmates. However, she was clear in her response to Stan that she had not meant her social capital to be built at the expense of Francine, the girl from Cameroon. In her justification to Stan, she exonerated herself by aligning with Francine as an African, as family. She implied that her way of talking was something that one racial family member did with another and stated she had no other interest in mind.

How students argue against teachers' definitions of problems can provide insight into students' stakes, when stake is thought of as the amount of interest or claim the person has for that position. In Sonandra's case, she had much more at stake in not being seen as unkind to the girl from Cameroon than in being thought to be flirting with Brock.

By telling Sonandra that her signifying with a classmate from Cameroon was inappropriate, Stan moved to protect Francine and to keep Sonandra from repeating that style of talk. Stan's stake was in defending those students who did not have the personal or social confidence to withstand what he viewed as "put-downs," those whose academic performance he assumed would be negatively affected. In this class, these were, in addition to Francine, a little person[24] and Arab American students who did not engage in cross-race signifying. Stan believed that the put-down as a means of building social relationship and social capital was counterproductive to students who were reading their personal writing aloud and talking about personal experiences, both fundamental to his stake in his "real writing" curriculum.

Teachers and students frequently operate according to different purposes during classroom instruction. In this case we observed how differing purposes were discursively negotiated around a problem incident, as is often the case. In this instance, blaming was avoided and escalation prevented, even though racial identities and social relationship building among and across races were complicating factors. Both teacher and student were able to exercise authority and self-interest, even though stakes were at odds in the characterization of the problems. What the teacher said was directly related to his teaching stake in what was occurring. He wanted his classroom to be a learning community in which he believed students would be academically more successful, a stake we believe is common among teachers. The student wanted to save face, exert her identity, and build social relationships—all driving interests for most adolescent students. Interpreting what happened in terms of power circulation provides an explanation that can be the basis for useful action. At first the teacher exercised power in the relationship, and then it circulated to the student. In this circulation, both achieved their purpose and satisfied their stake.

Focusing More Directly on Race

We know that Stan and Sonandra's different social and racial worlds influenced what they said. They also influenced how each of them spoke. Stan and Sonandra spoke in different varieties of English. What Stan referred to as "put-downs" and "attitude" have been extensively described as Black oral performance language. They are elements of "signifying." Commonly engaged in by African American men, women, and children, signifying is a highly respected social strategy of verbal artistry. In its most animated form, it is a verbal game used to launch insults. In more subtle forms, it is often a way people in weaker positions play with language to deal with those in positions of power who do not understand the language play. Signifying can mean a number of things, including making fun of a person or situation, stirring up conflict, or communicating indirectly. African American women's signifying has been described as counter-language characterized by its baited indirectness.

Sonandra's performance of signifying was to her an ordinary and appropriate social way of being and acting. On this third day of class, she learned that Stan did not consider this way of talking appropriate social behavior. She engaged in the first of what would be hundreds of negotiations with him about her discourse—which is to say, how she spoke, gestured, and moved—with others in the classroom. Stan did not know about signifying. He could not possibly draw on African American oral traditions in his interaction with Sonandra. He could only speak from his position as a teacher authority and a culturally White male.

By comparison, Marita did know how to signify and rap, and frequently did so with her students. She chose to invoke a teaching discourse of authority in her interaction with Byron and Jacob. However, Byron and Jacob were playing to multiple audiences by moving in and out of AAVE and standard academic English. This was their way of sustaining their social authority as African American adolescent males in this situation.

We have only provided two examples out of thousands of possibilities concerning difference and race. We think it is important to consider an example with much younger students and another racial mix. No matter how many examples are provided, we could never address all the complications of negotiating race and identity. In Marita and Byron's situation, their interaction reminded us to consider whether and how students can have competing stakes in school discourses and in roles, and related identities, that are antithetical. In the transcript that follows, we will observe how a White, sixth grade girl negotiates competing stakes in relating to her African American classmates and her African American teacher. Her negotiations are complicated, as they were for Stan, by issues of dialect and social positioning through language.

In the following transcript, test preparation is the focus of the lesson. The teacher wants students to realize that test question language is a particular register for a particular audience and may not sound familiar. In order to help students negotiate extra-formal test question language, the teacher helps students recognize that we speak in different ways for different purposes with different audiences. To make her point, she invites students to consider how they speak with their friends versus how they might speak with a principal or parent.

As you read this transcript, notice how Joyce and the teacher work in tandem to position Joyce as an accepted member of the group and how complicated these moves become.

Transcript 12.4

MS. E.:	What's meant by that
	I need to know what the word dawg means
	What is that
JOYCE:	(Spoken slowly) Hi friend
STUDENT:	What?
MS. E.:	Hi friend
STUDENT:	[XXXXX
MS. E.:	Also when you use the word dawg on the end
	You're saying
	[hi friend

At this point in the transcript, Ms. E. has invited Joyce to give the answer to what *dawg* means. Joyce has given that answer and Ms. E. confirms that answer to the class. However, the class loudly disagrees.

STUDENTS: (Shouting disagreement)

MS. E.: Oh shhh

S'cuse me

S'cuse me

MS. E.: Alright

What's her interpretation

Her interpretation is

It means hello friend

So you mean the word dawg is actually a friend

STUDENTS: (Students call out and loudly disagree)

MS. E.: When I call you a dawg

That's a friend=

Ms. E. recognizes that the students are dissatisfied with Joyce's interpretation of dawg. She tries to address their concerns by restating Joyce's explanation. However, aware that she is out of alignment with the rest of the class, Joyce suddenly becomes unsure of her answer.

JOYCE: =I don't know

STUDENTS: (Students continue to disagree but more quietly)

MS. E.: Oh you

Okay=

JOYCE: =I'm WHITE

Confronted by the continued social disapproval of her classmates, Joyce breaks away from the teacher's attempts to align her with the African American students. Instead, she reads their disapproval as a call for her to declare her Whiteness. Her peers won't permit her to define a term that they use outside of school, so she takes their cue and essentially says, "I'm White. How would you expect me to know exactly how you would explain it?"

Another facet of this interaction is that Joyce's definition of the word "dawg" is not discernibly different from what her peers were suggesting. This is partly what led to an interpretation that the issue was more about who was entitled to define a socially used term and who wasn't.

Next when Joyce rejects Ms. E.'s help to reposition her in relation to her classmates, Ms. E. finds herself out of alignment with her African American students. This is a threat to Ms. E.'s status as both a teacher who must maintain order and an African American woman who wants to align with her students. In response, Ms. E. invokes her identity as a racial insider by referring to sisters. The class resists and Joyce protects herself.

Transcript 12.5

MS. E.:   Well you hang out with some sisters

            So do you really know

STUDENTS: (Students continue to resist)

JOYCE: I'm white

Neither Joyce nor Ms. E. are recognized by the class in the ways they want to be.

By looking closely at these transcripts, we observed the striking rapidity and tenuousness with which identity and social relationships were reinforced, constructed, and deconstructed in interactional moments. We can note that classroom conditions for teaching and learning were strongly influenced by how teachers and students used and accepted ways of talking, how through these discursive conditions they positioned each other, and how these positionings contributed to or diminished conflicts. Conflicts, as an inevitable element of classroom life, are tied to the purposes of individual interactants. Understanding how and why they occur can provide insight into how teaching and learning are productively and interactively managed in multiracial and multicultural classrooms.

Taken together, these three cases illuminate *difference* through the framework of discourse we provided in Part 1. Broadly drawn racial and social distinctions that mask the complicated work of classroom teaching and learning cannot stand when teachers understand the work performed by the interactions they engage in with their students. The three cases demonstrate how identity, social relationships, and social life are always under construction in classrooms. They illustrate how teachers and students call forth various expressions of race during acts of teaching and learning as purposeful types of talk. The cases make apparent that in classrooms race is a social relationship, a personal identity, and an academic practice that is discursively constructed. As such, race is influenced by and influences the normative classroom conduct of teachers and students (Rex, 2006).

What Does This View of Difference Mean for the Classroom?

The lens we have presented in Part 3 can lead us to a more nuanced and transportable understanding of how individual interactions contribute to the normative conditions in a classroom as they accrue over time. As illustrated in this chapter, this lens also makes it possible for teachers to productively distinguish between disagreement and conflict in managing difference successfully. Within classroom interactions, whether within or across race, disagreement is inevitable, but conflict is not. By sorting out with their students what is occurring, teachers can manage disagreement so that it does not become conflict and hijack learning. These descriptions of "the problem" are strongly shaped by a person's stake, and understanding what is at stake for students can provide teachers with more options about what to say and when. These options become visible when teachers understand that their stake influences how they view the person with whom they are speaking and the situation in which they are engaged. How they view them shapes how they attribute accountability. To whom they attribute accountability leads to exoneration or to blame.

Race is one aspect of self-interest and so of stake—as is ethnicity, social class, and all the other classifications of social group identity that people take on to characterize themselves. Negotiations of self-interest among teachers and students involve within- and across-race discourse marked by competing purposes for building and sustaining relationships, identity, and subject matter. Difference is the condition, similarity is the default defense against conflict, and negotiating difference is the way to achieving moments of elusive and short-lived equilibrium. Negotiating difference means that as they interact, teachers and students discursively construct the problem, a way of talking about it, and the resolution (e.g., conflict, truce, acquiescence, or agreement). They are constructing their own and the other's public, classroom identity and the view of subject matter that counts. They are also determining the boundaries of description and engagement. Masterful handling of disagreement and management of stake mark the successful learning-centered classroom.

Once teachers understand themselves and their students in respect to difference, they can negotiate agreeable compromises. Negotiation is not a concession. Rather, in that negotiation, power is circulated, which is what keeps open teaching and learning opportunities.

Part 4

Accountability and Assessment

Introduction

Up to this point we have promoted teachers' analysis of their interactions with students, focusing on the outcomes of their utterances to help them align their instruction with their intentions. We limited our focus so that teachers could experience a sense of their own agency in improving their teaching. In this part, we expand the scale of our focus to include the issues of accountability and assessment. We maintain that examining interactions with students in the ways we have illustrated is a means of professional accountability and assessment. Teachers can hold themselves accountable by assessing the interactions in their classrooms. However, as we know only too well, currently this method is neither the only one nor the most influential for evaluating teaching. To put the individual agency of teachers into perspective given today's education climate requires another dimension—accountability beyond the individual teacher. No Child Left Behind legislation and high stakes testing have ushered in an era of school and teacher accountability as a political and public concern. Adequate yearly progress has become a measuring rod for student and school performance, and teachers have become lightning rods for blame when test-measured progress is not achieved.

These conditions complicate the goal of maintaining alignment between one's teaching intentions and instruction. For example, Lesley's research has demonstrated that test preparation can compromise teachers' best intentions and teaching practices (Rex & Nelson, 2004).[25] Her work raises the question: How can teachers apply discourse analysis methods and approaches to become aware of classroom interactions that have the potential to undermine their curricular objectives? When schooling outcomes across the nation are assessed through standardized tests, how can teachers prevent themselves from being swept up in the language of testing and a narrowed test preparation curriculum? How can they avoid the subtle erosion of practices we know serve students' learning of complex knowledge not measured by tests?

In Part 4, in addition to revisiting the constructs of **identity** and

alignment presented in the Curriculum and Difference sections, we will apply the additional concepts of **agency, efficacy,** and **reframing** as they relate to reinterpreting and repositioning testing. These constructs make it possible to observe how teachers can build and sustain rich curricular opportunities through an awareness of positioning and circulation of power. In Chapter 13, we look closely at student–teacher interaction to illustrate repercussions for students and subject matter when teachers are unaware of how test pressures position them. In Chapter 14, we examine the discourse of test prompts to observe how high stakes language can be rewritten and reinterpreted to frame more agentive thinking and writing. Chapter 15 demonstrates how staff developers wrote curricular units for test preparation that repositioned teachers and students in relation to testing, and how these texts circulated power among stakeholders.

Before launching into these chapters, we rehearse some of these concepts through an experience Lesley had when she invited teachers to participate in an action research project. The teachers had been struggling with the accountability measures enforced by their district to raise test scores, and they thought Lesley was a district informer.

As Lesley recalls:

> The teachers were in their second year of teaching without a contract, and I was an outsider from the university. Contract negotiations had derailed, their superintendent and principal were demanding accountability, and I wanted to record what they did in their meetings and classrooms. I was beginning a study of how the teachers interacted with their students. I was looking for teachers who would be my research partners in using the information we collected to help them understand how their interactions generated learning. As I explained my interest in observing their classrooms, some stared and some looked away. When I asked for questions, few spoke.
>
> I spent the next few months finding out why my reception had been so chilly. Besides being viewed as a spy for the district, I was regarded as a university person with an agenda, as a White woman in a predominantly African American district, who could not understand their situation, and as a stealer of their already limited time—one more district-engineered bright idea to improve student achievement.
>
> I recognized my situation in Deborah Meier's commanding descriptions. I had read her book, *In Schools We Trust,*[26] where she chronicles the negative effects of mistrust in schools in the current policy era of testing and accountability. The testing juggernaut has created an atmosphere of tension and distrust that makes it difficult for people to engage. It is a Catch 22. There is insufficient trust to engage, and without engagement we cannot build trust.
>
> The teachers I faced were living with the same issues. They were

besieged by demands for accountability, mostly through improved standardized test scores. They no longer had the strong support of their community or their students' parents, and they felt powerless. In meetings called and run by the more powerful, such as this one, they managed the most sensible way they knew how—through silence and passivity. Under these circumstances, passive resistance permitted agency, which allowed them to save face.

Though I might have wished for a more positive initial introduction, that first meeting could not have been different. The stakes of all in attendance were at odds, and the circumstances did not permit immediate productive engagement. However, between that meeting and the next, teachers spoke with others who had worked with me. They repositioned me in alignment with the teachers in supporting the growth of their practice. Over the next several meetings, the teachers and I were able to talk in ways that circulated power among us so that they experienced a sense of their own agency. I was no longer positioned as the only powerful person in the room. The teachers and I co-constructed me into a safer and more useful resource.

To be productive when we met again, all of us needed to co-construct our identities as we talked with each other. Once word got around the building that I was in alignment with teachers and not an administrative spy, the teachers could trust me enough to talk. Once we were talking we could begin negotiating identities, stake, and status. Even though for a considerable time they remained wary of my intentions, through continued interaction joint reconstruction of identities could be comfortable for both parties.

In any school context we need to hold open conversational opportunities for such co-constitution. If our conversation hadn't permitted that reconstruction, productive social relationships and collaboration would have been inhibited. Each year thereafter, every time a new teacher or administrator came into the district, we had to consciously hold open opportunities to reconstitute identities and productive social relationships.

Lesley and the teachers learned from their complicated early meetings that all of us take on different views of ourselves in social relationship as we co-construct our identities. Conversations between Lesley and the teachers became careful and purposeful because they were aware of how they were positioning one another. At the same time, their awareness of the importance of outside pressures led them to carefully negotiate what counted as significant knowledge of these pressures in these conversations. Social recognition of each other enhanced a sense of power in their right and ability to be agentive rather than passively resistant in the face of institutional and political accountability.

Outside pressures are important for everyone, no matter what age or in what role. Recalling Marie and Danny from our discussion of identity, worlds, and interdiscursivity in Chapter 6, we understand that Danny's schooling world told him he was not a competent reader. Marie's schooling world told her she was responsible for helping Danny become a competent reader. Knowing that these two world views existed, Marie assumed that when Danny lied about giving his mother the note and doing his reading homework, he did so to save face. His lying is comparable to the silent treatment exhibited by the teachers when they first met with Lesley. By lying about the note and his homework, Danny was also agentive in protecting his identity in his schooling world. Marie knew that she and Danny could construct a new reader identity and schooling world for Danny only if they could sustain their interactions. She understood that language constitutes who we are and the worlds we inhabit.

Marie intentionally spoke to align with Danny's world. She kept the conversation open. To do so she had to overlook Danny's discursive action—lying—which at that moment was inconsistent with what it meant to be a reader. From Marie's actions, we learn that she stayed focused on the reader identity she wanted Danny to assume, rather than on the non-reader identity Danny's actions promoted. Had Marie been following the conventional teacher script, she might have chastised Danny for not doing his reading homework and for lying about it. However, she knew that Danny's school world shaped and was shaped by his identity as a non-reader. He was acting as he had learned to act to sustain his identity and sense of self when asked to read. Marie's moves illustrate that with interdiscursive awareness teachers can consciously rewrite teaching scripts. They can productively focus on the identity they want students to assume through the ways they talk with them. Eventually, Marie and Danny were able to recreate Danny's identity. He became a reader who was reading at grade level because of Marie's awareness that language influences the worlds and identities teachers create.

Chapter 13

The Discursive Qualities of Inclusive Diverse Classrooms

For the last fifteen years, as Lesley has studied teaching practices in classrooms, she has observed students with language differences, social conflicts, or learning disabilities engage and achieve. In these studies, she documented how students with disabilities, with English as a second language, and with nonstandard English varieties successfully interacted in instructional practices. Similarly, in other classrooms, students tracked as general students were able to succeed in classrooms designated for the "gifted and talented." That work has led us to look at the discourse practices of those classrooms to understand what, in their practices, may have contributed to the students' achievement. The role of the teacher's language-in-use was always central. However, understanding how language outside of classrooms also influences the worlds and identities evoked and created in the classroom was also key. Interdiscursivity—that is, how discourses intersect, overlap, and interlace—is ever-present in all classroom discourses, whether it is spoken, written, or acted.[27]

Before High Stakes Test Preparation

The language of high stakes testing has had a powerful influence on the world of schooling and on teaching.[28] What is available for teachers to say and how they frame what they say are constrained by conversations among policy makers and administrators. Before test preparation language and accountability pressures dominated, discourse performed in particular ways in the classrooms Lesley studied. When she compared the discursive practices in these classrooms she noted five commonalities.

In each classroom, diversity was regarded as a resource for opportunities to learn something valuable. During lessons, all points of view and ways of expressing them were respected. Also, the standards for academic achievement provided a wide range of possible performances. No single way of producing knowledge was privileged over another. Sometimes students represented their understanding in drawings. Other times they wrote, acted, or videotaped. Closely related to academic achievement was a flexibility toward what constituted "academic" performance. For example, a student with learning disabilities would be considered successful and affirmed for asking a question that may have been less conceptually sophisticated or articulately expressed than a question asked by a student classified as "gifted and talented." Additionally, in these inclusive classrooms, the way students talked about themselves as students and the ways they went about the work of being a student were included in interactions about academic expectations. How various students did homework and the roles of parents and social communities in supporting student work were integrated into talk about academic tasks. Students' personal texts were a legitimate part of the curriculum. The stories they told, the personal narratives they wrote, and the anecdotes and allusions they included as evidence for their choices and arguments became part of the interdiscursive textuality of the classroom. Teachers and students referred to these texts across the semester in ways that reminded them of the ideas and knowledge they had constructed.

After High Stakes Test Preparation

After high stakes testing became the measure of student academic accomplishment and teachers assumed responsibility for test preparation, Lesley's research revealed a disquieting transformation in these classroom interaction commonalities. Meanings for diversity, performance standards, and performance stances narrowed, and students' selves and their personal texts disappeared. Diversity was framed as a limitation and redefined as student deficits that required scaffolding in order to learn the discourse of the test. The standards for academic achievement grew much narrower. The earlier wide range of possible performances to display knowledge and understanding were no longer allowed. Teachers assisted students in taking specific, procedural, and rubric-driven stances toward what constituted academic performance. Not unexpectedly, student references to how they went about doing their work in and out of school disappeared from the discourse as did their personal texts. Their personal narratives disappeared as well, to be replaced by genres appropriate for testing.

Instructional Discourse After Test Preparation: An Illustration

In the following interaction, we mean to illustrate in concrete terms the kind of discourse patterns that can take hold in classrooms dominated by test preparation mandates. We return to the interaction between Marita and Nathan (from Chapter 4) as an example. We do not mean to suggest that this incident alone undermines inclusive learning. The interaction is presented to illuminate how, as they accumulate over time, instructional moments contribute to often unrealized and unintended conditions. To understand other discourses, with their values and beliefs that speak through Marita's language-in-use, it is important to know that Marita had gained access to middle-class life by becoming proficient in standard English. An African American from the inner city, on her own since the age of fifteen, she had earned two M.A. degrees. She was proud of her accomplishments and considered her schooling, especially the interventions of her teachers, central to what she considered her upward social and career mobility.

This test preparation exercise had come after a series of activities about *Go Ask Alice*, a 1970s novel about a teenage girl's descent into drug addiction. In an animated debate in response to Marita's question, *What influenced Alice to avoid her problems?* students referred to places in the text in order to blame either Alice's mother or father. Through such discussions, and directed journal prompts (such as *What do you wish your parents knew?*), Marita had directed students to compare the character's issues to their own. Marita encourages this type of thinking. She wants students to think about the actions of the characters and themes in the books they read by comparing them to their life experiences and by challenging their thinking about what is best, right, and healthy in life.

Before the interactional episode, Marita had been leading her class through a paragraph writing exercise in preparation for their high stakes test. She had prompted her students' writing by asking them if drugs affected them, their families, and communities the way they affected, teenaged drug-addicted Alice. Using a graphic organizer, students were to write sentences in boxes representing sentences in the paragraph. The interaction that follows occurred as Marita walked around the class, silently assessing students' topic sentences.

In this segment of talk, Marita and Nathan, an African American sixteen-year-old from the inner city with poor performance scores in written English, are discussing his topic sentence. Marita and Nathan clearly have different views of what to accomplish to improve the quality of his workmanship. Nathan begins by paraphrasing what he means by the sentence he has written (1), and Marita responds to what he has said by challenging its veracity with, *That wouldn't be true though* (2). Nathan argues back by giving evidence that warrants his argument (3). Unlike Alice, his whole community stays together and is drug-free because they are athletes.

When he corrected his prose, or crafted his writing, Nathan worked to improve its effectiveness. For example, earlier in the term when he had written about the "real world" applications of the lyrics in Stevie Wonder's song "Pastime Paradise," Marita had congratulated Nathan for drawing from his own life and from television and movies to *tell it like it is* in AAVE-laced prose.

Transcript 13.1

1. NATHAN: Ok what I'm saying drugs doesn't affect me and my family and my community.

2. MARITA: That wouldn't be true though.

3. NATHAN: It is true. Where I live we say no to drugs. The whole community we all stay together and we are drug free 'cause we all 'r athletes.

4. MARITA: (She silently reads Nathan's sentence (.5) before rephrasing it.) The way drugs affects Alice (.5) does not affect my family, friends, or community. That's how it should [sound.

5. NATHAN: [And I'm going to explain why. I'm gonna explain [why

6. MARITA: [Okay. Did you hear what I just said? What did I just say? The way drugs affect Alice=

7. NATHAN: =does not=

8. MARITA: =Wait. Listen. (She reads his sentence) The way drugs affect Alice they don't affect my family friends and community. Is that how you talk?

9. NATHAN: I'm gonna say does not.

10. MARITA: [Is that how you talk?

11. NATHAN: [I'm gonna say does not.

12. MARITA: Answer the question. Is that how you talk?

13. NATHAN: Uhuh.

14. MARITA: Okay. Then you need to reread before you=

15. NATHAN: =uhuh. Okay=

16. MARITA: =Read it. Okay. Write it like it should be.

17. NATHAN: Uhuh. Okay.

However, in the present interchange, Nathan and his writing are being treated differently. He is not a writer, but a student who is getting it wrong. His writing should be the way it is supposed to be for the test. On one level, we could say that Marita was doing what any good English teacher should be doing—correcting a student's incorrect grammar and telling him to be self-correcting. These are central skills for good performance in the world as well as on the test. However, we selected this moment because it so powerfully demonstrates how Marita's best intentions to teach what students must know and do unwittingly stymied her goal of keeping students like Nathan, who do not perform well on academic tasks, engaged in the learning of the class. This interaction possibly undermined Nathan's future engagement because it was one of many similar moments throughout the term, moments that in isolation seem innocuous, but when they accrue can undermine engaged participation.

Having already built the expectation that in this class Nathan's personal life is central to what he thinks about as he reads and writes, this shift to a much narrower range for defining performance more tightly inscribes who he can be as a writer. Marita speaks as though there is no flexibility in what constitutes correct performance. She does not permit Nathan's point about the difference between Alice's and his community's involvement with drugs to be a part of the discussion. She is more concerned about the syntactical structure with which he expresses his proposition. Her response positions Nathan's personal story as material for practicing paragraph writing on-demand, and thus diminishes its importance. Since Nathan takes great pride in his abstinence from drugs, his insistence on explaining tells us that he reads Marita's reaction as dismissive of his identity. As her interchange with Nathan demonstrates, Marita's concern for her students' learning the discourse of the test eclipsed her interest in her students' thinking and lives. This move prevented their stories, and the identities those stories represented, from becoming part of the learning in ways that built and sustained engagement.

Nathan and Marita's interchange, when viewed in relation to the usual talk in this class, shows us how test preparation lessons can conflict with instructional practices calling for personal connections and complex thinking which effective teachers have long employed. Marita thought she was integrating test preparation into her regular instruction, when in fact her regular practices were co-opted by the discourse of test preparation. She had no idea that her discourse practices to accommodate test preparation had compromised her curriculum.

Prior to test preparation, Nathan had learned to see writing as not only an expression of an identity he wanted to share, but also a medium for creating an identity that could be socially acknowledged. Nevertheless, in each instructional interaction, Marita had to make a choice. To do what was best for Nathan, what should she focus and spend time on? Her choice in the interchange was to cut nonacademic conversations short. Marita's concern for Nathan to succeed on the test led her to instruct him to write as she believed test scorers expected. There was no time to discuss how Nathan's community supported its young people as athletes and maintained a drug-free environment. It was more important for Nathan to practice writing in academic standard English. When what counts as expression, as being a writer, and as being a member of the class are collapsed to fit the high stakes frame, the classroom conversations that engage students such as Nathan in school writing disappear. We view this as a critical dilemma that teachers need to thoughtfully address in analyzing their interactions, because when these conversations are dropped, their students most at risk of failure are more likely to disappear from their classrooms.

Even when teachers are conscious that they are narrowing their curriculum, they cannot exist outside of pervasive discourses of schooling in the world. Accountability and testing discourse is framing a whole generation of teachers and teaching. Dealing with this challenge means being aware of the ways in which prevailing testing discourses narrow instructional choices. Teachers should examine the assumptions embedded in particular accountability and evaluative assignments and measures and renegotiate the way they play out in their classrooms. They can move from "Prove to me that you know this or can do this," to sustained classroom engagements and interactions with text and talk as tools for learning and explorations of knowledge.

This discursive repositioning and social alignment, from prove-it-to-me to let's-figure-this-out, is how students come to believe they are smart and can perform in effective ways; it is also how teachers come to believe they are respected professionals. We all feel more efficacious when we can make choices that satisfy our own and others' expectations for performance. If our choices are passive and reactive, we are more likely to feel powerless and ineffectual. In the face of intimidating pressures, students and teachers need more than ever to be agentive. By consciously choosing to assess and alter language, teachers can reposition themselves and their students through interaction. They can purposefully position and interact with students, colleagues, and administrators to affect how policy mandates get taken up.

Chapter 14

Interrogating Timed Prompted Writing in Professional Development Communities

In Chapter 13, we discussed how, through altering their discourse, teachers could change the **position** from which they and their students negotiate testing and learning, especially for students whose familiar cultures are not school congruent.[29] We observed how, under pressure, and even with the best of intentions, teachers cannot always be aware of the choices they make, of the alternatives available, or of their implications. This is true whether the discourse is spoken or written. In Part 1, when Marita challenged the truth of Nathan's statement that drugs are not a problem in his neighborhood, she was talking about the paragraph he had just written. This paragraph was the result of a graphic organizer Marita had drawn on the chalkboard. Five boxes, connected by lines, were presented in hierarchical order: the topic sentence box at the top, the three evidence boxes drawn below it, and the conclusion box on the very bottom. Marita had considered the graphic organizer a useful scaffold for test preparation writing, and it could have been. But the way Marita implemented the paragraph organizer, as we glimpsed in the excerpt with Nathan, limited rich interactions that support thoughtful development of student writing. Marita's discursive application of the organizer in her teaching served to limit possibilities for learning. With Nathan that was because she called up the everybody-is-influenced-by-drugs-in-the-hood discourse as well as others from beyond her classroom: accountability, standard English as a gatekeeper of academic achievement, and African Americans becoming successful within the dominant system. Over time, this **interdiscursivity** shaped what was possible for Marita and students to say and do in her classes. Marita's example informs teachers that they need to be vigilant of the interdiscursivity and the hidden assumptions in their teaching discourse. Without that awareness, teachers can inculcate the very discourses they believe compromise their best teaching.

Just as Marita was not aware of the multiple discourses she invoked as she utilized the graphic organizer, Richard (in Chapter 10) was unaware that his assignment emphasized assessable components for grading rather than his goal of encouraging complex understanding. Richard was assisted in analyzing his assignment to understand how its discourses and assumptions leaned more toward product than toward thinking. He could identify which discourses he had privileged in the language of his assignments—perform for a grade, produce a high quality school project, and learn history content as required by the curriculum. Subsequently, he could rewrite the project in language that prompted his students to produce more complex knowledge and understanding.

Richard's case illustrates how discourse analysis can be usefully applied to the written texts through which teachers communicate with their students. Every assignment comes with embedded assumptions that teachers need assistance in revealing. For Richard, and later for Marita, that assistance occurred within a professional development community of their colleagues, facilitated by a literacy leader able to use discourse analysis as a tool for understanding practice.

In this chapter we combine what we have learned about teachers' spoken discourses and the discourses invoked in teacher-produced written texts. In doing staff development within the test preparation climate, we also have had to be in conversation with accountability discourses and the ways in which they play out for teachers. Our aim in this next section is to look specifically at the language of test prompts and how teachers' own experience with prompted on-demand writing helps them to construct instructional opportunities. We take the stance that for teachers to find a balanced place for test writing practice in their curriculum requires an understanding of test writing. To be agents in preparing students to write to a test, without sacrificing effective curriculum for other types of academic writing, includes, among other elements, careful analysis of the discourse of writing prompts in relation to the writing situation and purpose.

We have found test prompt analysis to be an important skill for teachers because test preparation, across grades, involves test-approximated writing. Researchers report that in more and more classrooms, curriculum includes test-like prompts and occasions of timed writing (Hillocks, 2002; Gere, Christenbury, & Sassi, 2004).[30] Test practice, in which test-like prompts produce single drafts written under time pressure, call for the writer to marshal particular cognitive-specific text production processes. These processes differ from those marshaled when writers multi-draft within more flexible time and knowledge production constraints. In our professional development, before our teacher colleagues engage in creating curriculum and pedagogy, we observe together how what is said and written creates affordances and constraints for student knowledge-building. To effectively integrate test preparation into their curriculum, we worked with teachers to make visible the ways in which prompts position writers, their thinking, and their writing.

Prompting Pre-structured Timed Writing

We all agreed that persuasive or explanatory writing is a highly valued academic capability used by gatekeepers in many subject areas and grade levels. Once termed *transactional writing* (Barnes, Britton, & Rosen, 1969)[31] and infrequently assigned, we discussed how frequently formal and informal versions of this type of writing appear in classrooms and on tests. Knowledge from the fields of composition and rhetoric, as well as the teachers we worked with, informs us that to produce credible and felicitous writing in this manner calls for carefully and critically considered ideas, reasoning, and execution. It is rarely produced in 30–60 minutes, even with instructional support. In our professional development communities, using a protocol for discourse analysis, we asked teachers to consider how test writing prompts position writers and the writing they produce, and how that influences instruction. We asked them to consider whether test writing requires the same knowledge and facility as less time-urgent writing.

To answer our question, the teachers began by analyzing three different kinds of writing prompts. In the demands they made of the writer, they represented the common types of prompts that appear in on-demand, single-draft test essay writing.

On-demand Writing Prompts

The first prompt invokes a personal narrative organized to illustrate an important point by asking the writer to recall and organize an illustrative memory.

1. *Describe an experience in which you learned something important from someone else.*

The second prompt requires writers to define a construct by drawing on their memories.

2. *How would you define leadership based on your life experience?*

The third prompt calls for an argument to convincingly persuade.

3. *Recent polls have found that people obtain more of their national news from Jon Stewart's fake television news program,* The Daily Show, *than from regular news outlets. Should we be concerned about citizens getting their news from comedy news shows?*

We analyzed the language, syntax, and meaning of each prompt to determine how it made a particular request of writers, which resulted in circumscribed types of writing. We discerned that the prompts, given the time constraints of the test situation, led to the production of a particular genre of test writing—functionally efficient, stand-alone drafts. The way the prompts are written in turn "prompts" writers to quickly organize their thoughts and produce a single line of argument. The first one asks for an event from memory from which the writer learned something of importance. Calling for a described event from the past, the prompt invokes a narrative genre in first person with a final point. The quality of the essay rests in the ability of the writer to tell a good story that implicates the lesson learned. The second prompt asks writers to build an abstract construct from their real life experiences. Though the prompt calls for memories from the past, the memories are not privileged as they are in the first prompt; rather, the writer's definition of leadership takes center-stage with the memories serving as specific illustrations of aspects of the definition. Narrative is no longer implicated as the organizational structure. This prompt invokes an expository structure, intended to explain and justify through targeted illustrations. The third prompt also calls for an exposition, but of another kind. Writers are asked to consider two opposing points of view already defined for them. The positions have been pre-formulated, so that the writer needs to provide evidence and warrants for one of the positions, as well as counter-positions. The work is in creating the evidence so that it speaks to the selected position.

All three of these genres—narrative lessons, definition, and persuasive argument—are forms of writing and thinking commonly taught, as well as commonly tested. When these forms are invoked, they organize writers' thinking into pre-structured formats that target *how* they write more than *what* they write. Such scaffolding assists the cognizant writer in writing quickly and efficiently, which in a testing situation is the dominant skill. On-demand prompts such as these become problematic when they are emphasized throughout the school year to the exclusion of other assignments in which time and efficiency are not privileged over complex thinking. As writers, we understand that much of the work of good writing takes time. Complex thinking, and the writing it inhabits, is built through planning, drafting, and revising text, and often occurs before the writer decides upon a stance, a structure, or a genre for the final essay. It is "considered" writing, often involving personal investment in considering other sources of information and ideas, wider and deeper reading on the subject, and experimenting with perspective, voice, and tone appropriate to the content, perspective, audience, and purpose.

Let us consider the first prompt as one example of how to approach writing from a "considered" as compared to an "on-demand" approach: *Describe an experience in which you learned something important from someone else.* Considered complex thinking to discern what is important about what one has learned requires the writer to try on various ideas and discard those less relevant to the essay and to the reader—a key rhetorical as well as conceptual process. Describing an unpleasant experience is not particularly difficult, as it is a common discourse narrative in everyday life. What *is* difficult is considering what one learned from that experience and writing the narrative of the event in a way that successfully illustrates why the writer came to the final understanding. With consideration such as that, students make a challenging conceptual leap from narrative to expositional theoretical speculation.

If there was time to think before writing to this prompt, teachers could encourage reflection by explaining that "importance" is not the same for everyone or for all occasions. They could pursue a line of thinking based on the assumption that importance is what is valued and believed to be vital at a given time for a particular person within particular social expectations. Such "consideration" of importance can deepen student writers' thinking about their relationship to the rest of their world, and expand their writing tools to encompass the complexity of the ideas they must sort through to produce a coherent essay. This is a very different thinking and writing process than writing on-demand from a single perspective, especially in a testing situation, which promotes off-the-top-of-the-head thinking and summative proficiency.

The purpose of on-demand writing is to demonstrate that the writer has command of standard English so as to take a stance and communicate an organized extended argument or explanation. Substance is what is needed to illustrate or support the organizing ideas. Originality, nuance, style, voice, and the power of the ideas are appreciated and will earn a high score. However, as many of us have found who have for years read these types of essays, the latter qualities rarely appear. Such prompts produce writing that rarely achieves our highest expectations. Writing teachers understand that generating the depth of thought, clarity of argument, and engaging style of writing that will earn the highest scores emerges for most student writers only after keen-eyed feedback and multiple revisions.

"On-demand" and "Considered" Writing Defined

In our professional development workshops we pondered what was meant by "on-demand" and "considered" writing, and how those two terms differentiated what students were being called to do to produce essays. We researched definitions of the words and discussed what and how the language in the definitions asked students to perform. In the box below, we have italicized the words and phrases that "on-demand" communicates.[32] Among them are: *difficult to ignore or deny, urgent requirement for time, resources, or action,* and *to require in order to function or succeed.* The sense of urgency to succeed by functioning immediately comes through strongly. In comparison, "considered" writing invokes a slower and more thoughtful process. Key words and phrases include: to *think carefully, to show respect, to weigh the pros and cons ... before making a decision on a course of action,* and *to examine ... and discuss ... in detail.* The teachers determined that considered writing calls for the need to examine and weigh multiple lines of argument and be respectful in what and how one writes to different points of view.

On-demand Writing

---

de·mand n
1. a clear and firm request that is *difficult to ignore or deny*

2. the level of desire or need that exists for particular goods or services

3. an *urgent requirement for time,* facilities, *resources, or action*

4. *a formal request that must be complied with by law*

v

1. vt *to request something firmly in a way that is difficult to ignore or deny*

2. vt to ask a question *in an extremely forceful way*

3. vt *to require* something such as time, resources, facilities, or action *in order to function or succeed*

Considered Writing

---

con·sid·er v
1. vt *to think carefully* about something

2. vt to have something as *an opinion or point of view*

3. vt *to show respect for or be thoughtful of somebody's feelings or position*

4. vt *to weigh the pros and cons of the situation before making a decision on a course of action*

5. vt *to examine* a problem and *discuss it in detail*

6. vt to take something into account, often in a sympathetic way

7. vt *to look at something carefully and with concentration* (formal)

Trying On-demand Writing

We asked the teachers to try out these two ways of writing. First, they followed a protocol (in the box below) to practice and analyze their on-demand writing. Half the members of the community wrote for twenty minutes to prompt #3. The other half partnered with a writer to takes notes on the process.

On-demand Writing Process Protocol for Teachers

The facilitator tells writers to read the prompt and begin writing.

After four minutes the facilitator says, "Stop."

The note-taker asks, "What were you thinking as you were writing?" For two minutes the writer explains and the note-taker records what is said.

After two minutes, the facilitator says, "Start," and the writer resumes writing while the note-takers elaborate their notes.

For the writer, this pattern of writing, stopping, reflecting, and restarting writing continues in the following pattern: 4 2 4 2 4 2 4 2 4 (four minutes of writing and two minutes of reflective talk).

Teachers who practiced this protocol regarded this process and the follow-up discussion as an eye opener. When note-takers compared their notes on the writers' processes, they observed distinctive similarities and differences. Writers who found a way to relate to the prompt began writing immediately and kept pen to paper to create argument and structure interactively and recursively as they wrote. They did not pre-plan. Some of the teachers who did not write, or who expended much of their time with idea generation, told us that they knew nothing about the topic or that it generated little interest. Participants consistently commented on the importance of observing that every writer followed a unique thinking and writing process. They observed that this experience complicated their assumptions about student readiness and the advisability of teaching students proscribed formulaic writing structures.

In the box below is a thirty-minute essay written by Michelle, one of the teachers who, regardless of the prompt, could always begin writing immediately. On the occasion of this essay, to raise issues of student readiness, we had constructed the prompt to simulate three conditions students often experience when they encounter on-demand writing prompts: They are unfamiliar or inexperienced with the topic; they find it a challenge to discern what they are being asked to write; and they are required to make an immediate choice that sets up what they will write. Michelle had never seen *The Daily Show*. Neither did she have any information about Rupert Murdoch. However, as an experienced and confident on-demand essay writer, she did not let this situation keep her from producing a full essay in the allotted time. She elected to believe that the prompt's information about Rupert Murdoch, with whom she was vaguely familiar, was accurate. She also elected to assume a stance provided by the language of the prompt. She would be *more concerned about who owns and controls news media*. She made this choice quickly and began writing, without consciously planning what she was doing and why. First she wrote the stance she would take in the first sentence and the reasons for this point of view in the remainder of the first paragraph. She followed with three body paragraphs and a final statement that restated her stance. Many of you will recognize the influence of the ubiquitous five-paragraph formula for essay writing.

Recent polls have found that people obtain more of their national news from Jon Stewart's fake television news program, The Daily Show, *than from regular news outlets. It has also been reported that many major media news outlets are concentrated under the ownership of one man, Rupert Murdoch. Should we be more concerned about who owns and controls news media?*

We should unequivocally be concerned with one man owning and controlling news media. Though fictitious news is bad for citizens to believe, controlled media is worse. With a controlled media situation, citizens are not given the option to make informed choices between right and wrong because all of the opinions, views, and beliefs stem from one source—in this case, Rupert Murdoch.

Rupert Murdoch has almost complete ownership of major media outlets: TV news, and radio news, primarily. Major media outlets are the primary source for most citizens to obtain valuable information about local, national, and international happenings. When citizens obtain information from news media, it is generally assumed to be correct and valid. However, many ideas, concepts and stories produced by the news are offensive because they come from a limited perspective. Take, for example, the images of Africa that are consistently shown on major TV networks. More often than not, citizens are portrayed as uneducated, impoverished and disenfranchised. This portrayal is disrespectful at best, erroneous @ worst. Unfortunately, this is the consistent image that American citizens get most often from the news media. It is not a coincidence that the main, repeated images come from the networks owned by one man.

In addition to the international portrayal, national problems persist when one source controls the mass media outlets as well. From Alaska to Wyoming, newscasters are all portrayed in one standard, cookie-cutter fashion: thin, attractive, classic "beauty" types deliver news from sunup until sundown. This is not accidental; clearly, networks have one "look" they strive to achieve. This look, however, is not reflective of the majority of American citizens. Coined as the "fattest nation in the world," clearly Americans do not fit into the standard mold shown by newscasters. People who do not have the "look" can feel left out and unwanted in their own country.

The most important reason why it is more dangerous for one person to control mass media is even more devastating than the first two. Mass media shapes our thoughts, beliefs and values. We are constantly bombarded with images and those images follow us throughout our days and create our opinions and cultural values. Black men are considered by many to be dangerous—not because they actually are, but because that is what they are portrayed to be. Young women are considered to be either power-hungry wenches or sex-kittens who succumb to men's wishes. Again, not because they are, but because that is how they are shown 2B. Inner-city schools are thought 2B dangerous dens of sexual promiscuity, inequity, sin and ignorance—not because they are, but because that is how the news portrays them to be.

Major news outlets are in control of shaping our thoughts, views and opinions. Americans are confronted with news stories on a regular basis. The images and ideas help craft our own personal beliefs. As such, it is dangerous to allow one man to have such a powerful influence—the influence over our minds.

Implications for Teaching and Learning Essay Writing

Although the teachers referred to the organizational structure of the five-paragraph genre when we asked them to explain what Michelle had written, we encouraged them away from that type of analysis. Instead, we asked Michelle to narrate for us the decisions she made as she wrote. Michelle's answers illuminated for teachers the decisions that produced a single draft with coherent reasoning. Few of those decisions related to the formal structure of the piece; that is, what to put where. Rather, the teachers realized that making sense had guided Michelle's writing, and that she had a great deal of experience with writing to make sense in a way that was persuasive for the reader. She had gained that experience through writing both on-demand and considered writing, and so had acquired the cognitive strategies to make sense in both genres.

We have discussed how timed, high stakes writing leads to particular cognitive and rhetorical choices. Making these choices as explicit as the choices writers make about structural organization is key to students being efficacious in their writing. Consequently, we asked the teachers to plan a teaching unit for considered writing: *Should we be concerned about citizens getting their news from comedy news shows?*—a prompt from which they had written another thirty-minute essay. The teachers discovered that using test-like prompts to produce considered writing made visible productive comparisons between the two writing situations. They could point out the differences between the two types of writing so as to improve their students' performances on each.

They emphasized that each occasion of writing called for different ways of reading the same prompt. For test writing the writer should focus on the particular genres and organizational structures that guide the writer's immediate thinking. In this case, the prompt asks writers to assume a stance and argue for their position. Teachers could analyze the language of the prompt with their students so as to take a stance (yes/no we should be concerned) and talk through the organizational structure they could follow. Then students could practice organizing their thinking within the proscribed genre while writing quickly. For students to be able to integrate persuasive reasoning into their fast writing they usually need practice of a different sort. Writing a well considered essay from the same prompt slows down the writing process so that students can practice and metaprocess reasoning. The disposition toward making persuasive sense takes time to teach and practice, as well as to learn so that it becomes as automatic for them as it was for Michelle.

Moving from fast to considered writing allows students (as well as teachers) to talk about what they are being asked to perform. Test situations require writers to retrieve information from memory or to creatively write "about" the topic. For instance, prompt #3 writers can recall the comedy news shows they have seen such as *The Daily Show* or *The Colbert Report*. Or, if they are unfamiliar with such shows, they need to hypothetically imagine what the effects of satirical news shows on their understanding of current events might be. Although substance counts, test evaluators are more interested in evaluating the writer's ability to create a sensible argument and to use written language correctly. A suitable English essay can be written by someone who has never seen a comedy news show, just as Michelle could write about the dangers of Rupert Murdoch with very little knowledge of his empire.

On the other hand, considered writing situations allow writers time to find information and to think about how to apply it. As the writing assignment for prompt #3 (in the box below) demonstrates, teachers can eliminate the need for quick memory retrieval and organization. In fact, in preparing for considered writing, early structuring is counter-productive. Immersion in substantive information and consideration of many possible stances before taking one is the writer's preferred strategy. The organizational structure of the essay emerges from the writer's best possible line of reasoning. First the teachers/writers are asked to watch an episode of *The Daily Show* to see an example of the kinds of shows referred to in the prompt. Then, they are directed to watch an interview with fake *Daily Show* newscaster, Jon Stewart. In this interview on the CNN show *Crossfire*, the two commentators challenge the usefulness of Stewart's interviewing of current politicians, and Stewart argues back. The third part of the assignment requires the teachers to find and read a commentary addressing *The Daily Show* or the writer's topic. This part of the assignment allows them to view how other writers have staged their stance and argument about the topic they are taking on.

---

1. Watch at least one episode of *The Daily Show*
http://www.comedycentral.com/shows/the_daily_show/index.jhtml

2. Watch the CNN *Crossfire* interview with Jon Stewart
http://www.ifilm.com/ifilmdetail/2652831

3. Read at least one commentary on either *The Daily Show* or the topic/stance you are taking.

4. Plan your teaching process to suit multi-draft writing.

By the time the teachers/writers reach step #4 in the assignment, they have sufficient information to understand firsthand the difference between writing quickly from experience and imagination about a topic and writing with substantive knowledge at their command. Without even writing the considered essay to prompt #3, they could predict the differences in teaching objectives and lesson planning that each type of writing invokes.

Original Academic Writing

As the teachers discovered, carefully considered as well as quickly written essays can evolve from prompts that invoke particular stances, reasoning, and genres of writing. Nevertheless, they realized that they should not limit their instruction to the teaching of considered essays from proscribed prompts. Worthy of time and teaching, but far more challenging are the rhetorical and intellectual demands of writing without a prompt. Figuring out what is worth writing about is an additionally important complex rhetorical and cognitive activity. Academic writing curriculum should also instruct students in the process of originating writing along with producing on-demand and considered writing. To limit written literacy schooling to teacher-created prompt-driven writing limits students' opportunities to interact discursively. These limits constrict students' agency and their possibilities for experiencing efficacy through the knowledge they bring to their learning. Classroom discussions limited to the teacher's point of view have a comparable effect of giving students the impression that only the teacher's knowledge and ideas count, and the disposition toward producing what they think the teacher wants to hear. Power cannot circulate, except within a proscribed field.

For students to experience being powerful in their writing beyond satisfying the demands of the current classroom situation requires the exercise of original writing. In the box below, we have italicized the words and phrases that "original" academic writing communicates. Among them are: *completely new, and so not copied or derived from something else, to invent something or bring something into being* and *departure from traditional or previous practice.* The language stresses a condition of experimentation and uniqueness.

Original Academic Writing

---

o·rig·i·nal adj

1. existing first, from the beginning, or before other people or things

2. *completely new, and so not copied or derived from something else*

3. possessing or demonstrating the *ability to think creatively*

4. representing a *departure from traditional or previous practice*

5. relating to or being something from which a copy or alternative version has been made

n

1. the first or *unique* item from which copies or alternative versions are made

2. a genuine work of art, and so *not a copy or forgery*

3. an *unusual* or eccentric person

4. a person of outstanding creativity or *revolutionary thinking*

o·rig·i·nate v

1. vi *to begin or develop* somewhere or from something

2. vt *to invent something or bring something into being*

Source: Encarta® World English Dictionary © 1999 Microsoft Corporation. All rights reserved. Developed for Microsoft by Bloomsbury Publishing Plc.

To better understand "original" academic writing, we applied our discourse analysis approaches to on-demand writing to serve as a base for comparison. On-demand writing, unlike original academic writing, gives students the opportunity to practice thinking and writing quickly. The single-draft writing that is produced is valued not so much for its originality or depth of thinking. Rather, what is valued is the ability to reflect a complete line of thinking in a grammatically and mechanically correct manner, in a short time period. Teaching on-demand writing requires teaching students to limit their reasoning to fit the knowledge and ideas they have at the moment of demand. They are not given time to read, discuss, and consider ideas and perspectives beyond what they can immediately access, as they would when generating original writing. Of necessity, the structure invoked by the prompt guides the writer's reasoning. For example, the prompt *Should we be concerned about citizens getting their news from comedy news shows?* pushes the writer to take one of two stances: "Yes, we should be concerned . . ."; "No, we shouldn't be concerned. . . ." These stances implicate predictable ways of reasoning; they are ways of organizing thinking so that ideas make sense to the writer and to readers. If we assume the second stance—"We should not be concerned about citizens getting their news from comedy news shows"—our line of reasoning is implicated for us, but not as a single structure.

This general line of reasoning could go something like this: The stance, "No, we shouldn't be concerned," implies a question: "Why shouldn't we be concerned?" Which in turn implies an answer, with a series of connected explanations: "We shouldn't be concerned because people who watch comedy news shows like *The Daily Show* with Jon Stewart do so because they find them funny. They find his funny because they are already aware of the news Stewart is referencing. They wouldn't watch the show if they were not already sufficiently familiar with the news to appreciate the humor. Because they watch we can assume that they appreciate the mockery." These three propositions are linked in a logical stream that constitutes reasoning: (1) People watch because they find the show funny; (2) people are already aware of the news the show references; and (3) people enjoy the mocking of the news. Each idea takes its sense from another idea it is linked to, so linkage in this particular order is what creates sensible reasoning. The order of the three ideas could be changed, but then the linkage between them would have to change to create another reasoning pattern. The point we want to make is not that the prompt predicts a single set reasoning structure, but rather that the range of options for what could count as sensible reasoning patterns is fairly tightly circumscribed.

Circumscribed reasoning in on-demand writing is privileged over more wide-ranging and experimental reasoning, found in original academic writing. Pre-thought constructs and reasoning patterns, because they are easier to access, are applied more often than original ideas and reasoning which take longer to create and link. There is not time for the exploratory work of writing—generating the substance of the writing, the perspective, the voice, and the genre. On-demand writing of necessity limits the thinking and consideration that we would expect of writers who have the time to produce considered writing. On-demand writing privileges a quickly assumed stance, accessible knowledge, pre-organized cognitive structures, and common discourses.

We agree that there is a place for on-demand writing in the curriculum.

However, we are concerned for students' development as writers when single-draft writing is privileged to raise test scores to the exclusion of opportunities to write and build understanding in multiple drafts and genres. We are also concerned when considered writing, which also belongs in academic curricula, is the alternative or only complement to on-demand writing. Considered writing does allow writers to explore relationships among writer, audience, purpose, and content without the burden of originating a stance. Nevertheless, because considered writing originates in a prewritten prompt, it circumscribes the range of appropriate reasoning patterns that can be assumed, also lightening the cognitive load. Even though considered writing expands opportunities for complex thinking beyond on-demand writing, student writers should have the opportunity of building a writing project from the ground up, with all the challenges that presents. With regard to instruction for original academic writing, teachers can scaffold a writing process that supports students in selecting a topic and developing a stance and a line of reasoning that has not been thought in quite that way by anyone else.

Analyses of on-demand, considered, and original academic writing can provide teachers with language and ideas with which to approach revising their curriculum. They can become more agentive in reframing test preparation writing as another genre in their writing curriculum. Looking closely at on-demand writing allowed the teachers we worked with to ask themselves what this form of writing provided and what it constrained in terms of instructional opportunities for students. As a result, teachers were able to incorporate on-demand, considered, and original academic writing throughout their practice.

Chapter 15

Reframing Accountability Measures: Repositioning Teachers and Students

This chapter deals with how agentive teachers can reframe their interactions with high stakes test preparation and reframe conversations around testing. First, we briefly report on a genre study of testing we developed as test preparation units.[33] Next, we illustrate how, when test pressures increased, we took working with the test in another direction. We leveraged overwhelming interest in the tests to draw attention to what counts as rich pedagogy and curriculum for all students. Borrowing Lucy Calkins' mini-lesson architecture,[34] we rewrote our test preparation units in language that changed the dynamic from helping students prepare for the test to helping teachers rethink and reframe their language of instruction, which in this unit was the language during test preparation.

Testing accountability culture became an opportune occasion. We had teachers' and administrators' attention. We could appropriate the discourse of raising test scores and preparing students for testing into a discourse of agentive teaching and learning that circulated power and afforded new instructional discourse. Testing became our opportunity, while improving instruction was our intention. Addressing current limited access—that is, the need for all students to experience sophisticated literacy practices, given the racial, ethnic, cultural, and economic diversity of student populations—became a central goal using the architecture of the mini-lesson.

Since 1998, when Lucy Calkins and her colleagues wrote the *Teacher's Guide to Standardized Reading Tests*, many of us have repositioned testing in our practice. We learned to conceive of testing as its own genre, giving it its due and containing it in a unit of study rather than letting test preparation infiltrate our entire curriculum. We taught students to approach the test in the same way we taught students about historical fiction, mystery, humor, realistic fiction, or any other genre. In repositioning testing, we also repositioned our students and ourselves from passive to active.

We offer an early lesson in our **Genre Test Unit** for Reading as an example of students analyzing the test to determine strategies that will work best for them.

One of the early lessons in the Genre Test Unit for Reading asks students to examine a test prototype and decide what things make it easy to read. Collaboratively, the students think through ways to adjust their reading when faced with challenges. After individually reading the test prototype:

1. Students talk in pairs about what in the test makes it easy to read.

2. The teacher charts their thinking for all to see.

3. Students are asked to decide what aspects of the test make it hard to read.

4. Again, students talk in pairs and the teacher charts their thinking.

5. The teacher asks students to decide how they would handle the reading difficulties they noticed.

6. Students talk in pairs and then the teacher charts their thinking so everyone in the class can see what to do when they encounter difficulties on the test.

Note the teacher role and the student role. This lesson is very different from having a teacher remind the class what to be mindful of and giving the students strategies to use when they are taking a test.

In this context, the students are trusted to come up with their own noticings of difficulty and to figure out strategies for negotiating text when it is difficult to read. The ownership for the ideas belongs more to the students than to the teacher. And, as previously noted, in the context of teaching and learning, ownership is a form of power.

Circulating power between teacher and students, students and students, and within professional learning communities as well, positions learners as capable and independent. The teacher/facilitator is a recorder of ideas. It does not mean the teacher may not insert her thinking into the conversation in case something important escapes the students' notice. However, the teacher makes space for student thinking and strategies and validates that thinking by making it visible on a chart to the entire group. Furthermore, the chart keeps track of group thinking and becomes a resource upon which to build additional strategies.

By studying the genre of testing, students became familiar with the format, test question language, multiple-choice answer strategies, and built the stamina necessary to concentrate for the length of the test. Test genre study repositioned students as test analyzers rather than simply test takers, so they felt confident and competent. Students' scores increased on state standardized tests the first time teachers applied these units.

The test genre activity reminds teachers that they have choices in how they position themselves and their students in a world of testing. They can choose a passive response or act in ways that build agency and voice for themselves and for their students. Over time, their actions shape their identities. The longer teachers and students remain powerless in the face of testing, the greater the likelihood of adopting identities that are reactive rather than proactive, passive rather than constructive. We know learning as an active, risk-taking endeavor. Passivity rarely leads to engagement and deep, internalized understanding.

Reframing a Larger Conversation

As a result of this limited success we began to ask ourselves whether it was possible to introduce previously silenced conversations into the discourse around testing. What happens to teachers' worlds, to those webs of interrelated discourses, when they find ways to speak back? Our opportunity came when the state revised the grade level tests and moved them from February to October. One issue to address was teachers' anxiety over getting their year underway, building community, and getting to know their students amidst immediate demands for test preparation. Teachers and students would begin the year saturated with testing discourse. In response, we decided to broaden the beginning-of-the-year discourse and make available new ways of interacting with testing. We created another generation of units of study to: (1) reposition teachers and students in relation to the tests so both were agentive; (2) contain test preparation so most of the school year could be devoted to high level teaching and learning; (3) level the playing field so that all students, regardless of socioeconomic status, had access to high quality, effective test preparation; and (4) simultaneously, raise the bar for what counted as quality instruction throughout the state, even in locales where staff development was an unaffordable luxury. In our minds, this was about linking test preparation and social justice.

Given a strong desire for equity and access across the state, we wondered if excellent instructional materials alone, even without staff development, could improve student learning. Furthermore, we wondered and worried if such materials would challenge or reinforce conceptions of scripted programs/materials that deskill teachers. Was it possible to write the test preparation genre study in such a way that power circulated among all stakeholders?

Discourse for Reframing

Colleagues Linda Denstaedt, Judy Kelly, and Laura set out to create genre units of study for the Michigan English/language arts test that would encompass all our goals.[35] They aimed to pull together the best test preparation ideas already available and organize and present them in ways that circulated power away from the tests and toward the teachers and their students. They planned to carefully analyze the test demands and create lessons tailored to the specific requirements of the state test.

Again, they found an example of the careful language they were looking for in the work of the Teachers College Reading and Writing Project. In addition to their testing as a genre study work, they borrowed from recent work on teacher talk during mini-lessons, the "Architecture of a Mini-lesson." By applying the mini-lesson framework they raised the instructional bar for many teachers and re-circulated power through altered discourses.

At one of her summer institutes, Calkins explained how she had asked her New York City staff developers to write up their mini-lessons to be organized into a series of books for teachers. When the lessons did not have clear teaching points, she and the Project Staff videotaped and transcribed numerous mini-lessons to determine how to achieve clarity. From that work came the *Architecture of a Mini-Lesson* as follows: (1) the connection [yesterday we . . .]; (2) the teaching point [today I'm going to teach/show you . . .]; (3) active engagement [students practice]; (4) the link [so, writers, now you know . . .]; (5) and the end of workshop share [re-teaching]. This work is always provisional and, even as we write, the Architecture is evolving. But the advantages of this protocol in classroom practice are many. For example, see **Introducing the Lesson,** in the box below, for a typical teacher discourse pattern that often leads into a lesson.

Introducing the Lesson: Example 1

Teacher: Who remembers . . . ?

Student 1: I remember. It's . . .

Teacher: Um hmm. Anyone else?

Student 2: And there's also . . .

Teacher: Very good. Who can add another idea?

Does the speech pattern sound familiar as you read Introducing the Lesson? It is more common in the elementary and middle grades than in high school. The teacher asks students to recall important information from a previous lesson or taps into prior knowledge to set up a current lesson.

Once the teacher has called on two or three students to reply, she often goes on to the point of the lesson for the day. So what are the advantages and disadvantages of this pattern? If the child is school congruent, that is White, female, middle-class, and an English speaker, following the thread of the conversation may not pose any challenge and the child may seamlessly follow the shared ideas through to the teaching point.

However, the more we learn about different discourses that shape our worlds, the more we come to appreciate that not all students are school congruent and many use discourse in ways that do not match school ways of talking. Hart and Risley's (2003)[36] study of the number of words spoken in the homes of children of poverty and wealth gives us pause. Not only are fewer words overall spoken in the homes of children of poverty, but the structures and forms of sentences differ dramatically from those experienced by children in middle- and upper-class homes. However, at the same time, we know from other research (Heath, 1983)[37] that students have rich funds of discourse knowledge. They bring to school language and social discourse practices that are either compatible or inconsistent with the discourse they are asked to use in classrooms.

Students' out-of-school discourses may include genres of talk, such as storytelling, that do not follow school patterns. Some students may use a different variety or dialect of English other than the standard. They may call out responses rather than raising their hands to be called upon. They may not make direct eye contact with an elder, because in their family it is considered impolite. Verbal language play or thoughtful discussions are valued highly in some families; in others, conversation about what has been learned from one's experiences is part of family life. In some families parents routinely ask "known answer" questions, while in others children are expected to take the floor in a conversation with adults when they have something appropriate to say. These children may find teacher-directed question and answer routines unfamiliar and disorienting.

The typical school discourse pattern in Introducing the Lesson may require some children to pay extra attention in order to process the flow of the conversation. For these children, by the time the teacher gets to the point of the lesson, the student may already have tuned out or lost the train of thought. Becoming aware that not all discourses privilege the same ways of using language resources helps us rethink classroom talk.

Compare the Introducing the Lesson example with another example that uses the Architecture of a Mini-lesson.

Introducing the Lesson: Example 2

Connection: Yesterday, readers, we learned to pay close attention to abrupt shifts in short stories. Those shifts remind us to stop and ask ourselves, what's happening here.

Teaching Point: Today, I'm going to show you how noticing shifts can help readers create theories when they read. Readers use shifts to create theories that help them understand the text.

[Teacher reads part of a short story and models her thinking by noticing shifts and creating a theory about what the shifts might mean.]

Active Involvement: Now, readers, turn and read aloud to your partner, pausing, like you heard me do, when you notice a shift. After the second shift, think aloud about your theory. Why that shift? Why in that moment? What could it mean?

[Teacher listens to students to find someone who can create and articulate a theory about the shifts in the short story.]

Link: So, readers, now you know that noticing shifts in short stories and thinking of theories about why those shifts and what they might mean helps you get involved in a text and builds understanding. When you're reading today I may ask you to share your theories with me.

Independent Reading: Reading under the influence of teaching.

Share: [Teacher finds one or two student examples that reinforce the teaching point. Teacher once again reminds students of the teaching point.]

So, readers, now you know, today and every day when you read, noticing shifts in short stories and thinking of theories about why those shifts and what they might mean helps you get involved in a text and builds understanding.

The lesson is intended to be part of a series, each lesson carefully built on the former, based on what the teacher notices that the students are able to do. The lessons are intended to be part of a longer unit of study, perhaps two to three weeks in length. Books have been written on this subject and by no means do we intend to reduce such rich work to a page or two. However, from a discourse perspective, we would like to point out aspects of this work that our colleagues have found extremely helpful in classrooms. Rather than fully flesh out each part of the architecture, we will provide only the framework's categories and supply examples of teacher discourse to make our points.

First of all, the teacher does not open the lesson with a question such as *How many of you remember?* or *Who can tell me?* By telling students what they will learn and why it is important, the teacher has moved to level the playing field. The students are not guessing what the teacher is thinking in order to duplicate the right answer. Instead, they are brought directly into a lesson that is modeled or demonstrated in some way.

In addition, right after the teacher demonstration, students practice the skill, often with a partner. The extra practice before independently trying on new learning supports those students who benefit from an additional rehearsal. Reading and writing are social acts and students are encouraged to try on new learning without risk of failure and judgment. Students are invited into a literate world in ways that are more likely to lead to success. They are positioned as competent learners and shown how to engage in literacy practices. Students and their teacher are part of a discourse community that values reading and writing. To avoid participation is to be left out, and children who view themselves as competent members of a group usually do not want to be left out.

Earlier, we wrote that our work derived from social constructivists, who study how individuals learn within a group, as well as social constructionists, who study how a group learns together. We think of the Architecture of a Mini-lesson as incorporating both approaches. The learner in the group is supported through demonstration, nonjudgmental scaffolded lessons, rehearsal, repetition, and talk.

These discursive supports allow students to participate as equals in the group without having to draw upon prior knowledge and cultural and academic experiences. Students are apprenticed into the literacy practices of a community that is forming through their participation. Practicing and modeling together, through the teacher's initiating and guiding discourses, is the social glue that coheres the learning community, which in turn shapes identities of literate members. Students are treated as readers or writers or thinkers, so when they practice reading, writing, and thinking, they become recognized as such. As capable theory builders, risk-takers, and competent learners, they share responsibility with their classmates and their teachers for the learning that takes place within the group. Power is circulated. Practice is built into the lesson structure. Independence as well as collaboration is highly prized.

Using the Architecture of a Mini-lesson, lessons are connected and designed to build up competence over time. Reading the mini-lesson in "Introducing a Lesson Revisited," teachers can imagine the lesson that came before, in part because the connection reinforces the teaching point of noticing shifts in short stories. They can also easily predict the subsequent lesson, though that would depend on how successful the students were in creating theories around shifts. They can anticipate the need to follow this lesson with a mini-lesson on supporting a theory with evidence from the text because often students offer inadequate evidence for their claims. They could imagine this series of mini-lessons in a larger unit of study on, for example, Reading to Make a Case or Making Sense of Reading, or Reading to Solve Confusion. Our point here is to note that the lessons are scaffolded in sequences within units that are explicit, guided, and reinforced.

Interdiscursivity was a strategic consideration in the design of these units of study. We utilized the architecture because of its effectiveness, but also because many support materials for grades K–8 were already available, especially for the elementary grades. Our alignment with published books, DVDs, and staff development opportunities encouraged teachers to try on the rich literacy work. Michigan test preparation and the *Architecture of a Mini-lesson* formed an interdiscursive coupling, each one borrowing from and re-inventing the other. What was now available to say regarding high stakes tests could transform into new teaching and testing practices. Teachers' need for help with our state test, particularly with the writing portion, reassured us that they would be listening.

As is to be expected, they listened and applied the units selectively. In schools where thoughtful discourse around teaching and learning was part of the culture, and where teachers and administrators collaborated and built trust with one another throughout the school year, testing was one more conversation among many. In those contexts, teachers did interact with the tests in more agentive ways and repositioned their students as analyzers of the tests. The bar for what counted as quality instruction, particularly with regard to test preparation, was raised in many locales across the state where the units were available. We are less certain as to whether or not the test preparation units freed teachers to focus on instruction beyond testing the rest of the school year. The stakes are so high that few administrators were willing to significantly reduce test practice, fearful of the consequences of lowered scores. Finally, we heard of too many instances where the units were handed to teachers without any explanation and teachers were told to use them for test preparation. Often, the schools with the fewest resources offered no support for teachers attempting to make sense of the complex instructional aims of the units. As with all teaching resources designed to deepen and transform current practice, the sense teachers make of the test preparation units depends upon their familiarity with the discourses in which they are written.

Epilogue

Interactional Awareness: A Few Words of Advice

Up to this point we have promoted teachers' analysis of their own discourse to help them align their instruction with their intentions. We limited our focus so that teachers could experience a sense of their own agency in improving their teaching. We have only touched upon the myriad societal, institutional, and political contextual conditions influencing what teachers can say and do, even in their own classrooms. We do not mean to undervalue their effects. For example, Jeannie Oakes' (1985)[38] body of work on tracking explains why, once placed in remedial tracks, students do not move out of them. And, through Shirley Brice Heath's (1983)[39] benchmark study of relationships between home and school literacy discourses, we understand why some students enter school more familiar with conventional classroom discourses. Such bodies of research and scholarship end once and for all the romantic notion that once teachers close their classroom doors they are left alone to construct the environment they want. We know being an effective teacher is not simply a matter of better observation of our classroom and being more agentive.

Nevertheless, we have focused on the relevance of discourse analysis for teachers to address what we consider to be three of the most important issues in education today: engaging students in the building of knowledge; respecting and incorporating diversity; and productively integrating testing and assessment into teaching and curricula. Some of you may be reading this book to improve your own and your colleagues' practice. Others may be professional teacher educators. No matter what your orientation, if we have succeeded in writing a useful book for educating teachers practicing in today's education policy environment, you will recognize some, if not all, of the approaches and methods we propose as applicable. Also, our argument in *Using Discourse Analysis to Improve Classroom Interaction* has been the importance of understanding that socializing, building significant relationships, and making knowledge meaningful are key to group engagement, participation, and learning. We consider that understanding necessary for becoming an effective and satisfied classroom teacher, whether as a twenty-something beginner or a seasoned practitioner. Once teachers adopt that perspective, learning how to analyze one's interactions with students and colleagues becomes highly effective. Even so, these methods do not succeed with one or two applications; rather, they require a long-term commitment to produce the kinds of results we want.

To encourage commitment toward this way of thinking and accompanying strategies, we suggest you take to your classroom, your students, and your colleagues the recommendations we have illustrated and implied throughout the book. Also, keep in mind that the best of instructional intentions can be sidetracked when we are unaware of the selves we create as interactions accumulate throughout a semester of teaching. We can be more effective when we remind ourselves, our students, and our colleagues that we are creating a teacher self as well as the selves of all those with whom we talk. By freeze-framing conversations over the course of a learning situation, whether in a classroom or a professional learning context, we can replay and reflect on numerous interactions to understand the "reality" these interactions represent; that is, the ways the people involved believe they need to act to be recognized as the type of people they want to be in that situation, and the kind of knowledge that counts as learning. With this insight, both novice and experienced teachers can choose ways to engage with others that either align with or disrupt the identities and knowledge that emerge in a particular learning context.

We have found the analogy of the old-fashioned flip-book helpful in making these often unfamiliar constructs more accessible. Hundreds of drawings, each only a slight movement different from the prior drawing, permit the reader to flip the pages to create a moving picture. The movie created by flipping pages quickly gives the appearance of action. The accumulation of actions tells a story. If teachers freeze-frame conversations, particularly those that raise thorny issues for them, over time, patterns will come alive. Some will be about students. How does a particular student want to be recognized? What self is she or he presenting? How is the teacher responding to that student? How are others in the class responding? Some could allow teachers to see what they and their students are presenting as important to learn and how each is responding. What is the teacher affirming as understanding? What student understanding does the teacher take up and how does she use it as part of the lesson? Does the teacher provide spaces for his students to learn together with and from each other?

Teachers can make dozens of metaphorical freeze-frame interactional flip-books for a single classroom. However, we suggest you only make a few from the interactions you think are key. In different flip-books, with other students and dissimilar interactions, you will create different but importantly related stories. This approach makes it much more likely that the meta-story we tell ourselves about who our students are as people and as learners, what they are learning, and how our teaching is going will be a good one. By "good" we mean the story will help us be more effective in our teaching, it won't push some students into unfair or unproductive positions, and it will help us as teachers grow in our practice. It is easy to jump quickly to stories based on too few freeze-frames; so being wary of that tendency is also important. Recruiting a colleague to observe one's classroom and teaching can be a fruitful means of disrupting problematic meta-stories, while distinguishing what constitutes helpful feedback.

We have learned that freeze-framing and flip-booking for patterns over time build the validity of teachers' stories and also develop their **interactional awareness**. With interactional awareness comes choice in what we and our students can say and how we respond to each other. Developing interactional awareness among teachers means they understand that, depending on the situation, learners want to be recognized by others as particular kinds of people. They believe that for learning to be successful, students need to feel they are capable of handling the academic challenge. They assume that how they construct their classrooms, the discursive choices they make, determines whether or not all their students will be perceived as capable and recognized as worthy of having something to say. They understand that at stake is student buy-in. Students want to know whether they have reason to engage. Is there anything in the course for them? Do they belong here? Are they a member of this community?

Such teachers are predisposed to replay conversations and reread assignments to ask themselves whether they are teaching what they think they are—a question that deters them from erroneously held assumptions. Ask yourself or tell your colleagues to ask themselves: What do I value in my instruction and assignments? What opportunities do students have to engage with the core issues that shape my discipline? When I assess my students, what is given most weight? Alert them to the limitations of continually asking students to interpret and replicate someone else's meaning as knowledge. Encourage them to show students how to critique texts as well as create their own texts, so they have the opportunity to establish their own authority. Depending on your classroom, you might ask your students to observe the written as well as spoken discourse, to determine what is privileged or valued. These strategies for analyzing talk and text can develop teachers and students' awareness of instructional opportunities and how to balance them.

We are teaching at a time when, in principle, universal education is a national goal. Diversity has never held truer. Special education laws regarding least restrictive environments are one of many influences changing the composition of today's classrooms. Students are more diverse racially, ethnically, linguistically, and socioeconomically than ever before. Yet, for the foreseeable future, the majority of teachers will remain White, female, and middle-class. How do educators work with these diversities in ways that are productive for learning? If teachers are to realize the ideal of education for all, then we must grow our understanding of our interactions with students and colleagues. What are we teaching? What is being learned? Who is doing the learning?

Interactional instructional practice, until recently, has been the domain of university researchers. Nevertheless, discursive pedagogy as an essential part of instructional practice has found its way into basic mainstream teaching and learning principles. The focus on interaction and discourse is being linked to the importance of reflection on practice, a common principle in teacher education, along with teacher research. It makes sense that reflection on social interaction in learning contexts and researching one's classroom interactions are the next step in this progression. If we have been successful in writing this book, our work has demonstrated that understanding social interaction in curriculum, instruction, and assessment holds promise for increased learning success with greater numbers of students. We hope you will share your insights from engaging with these approaches. Together, thoughtfully, with intentionality, we can increase **interactional awareness** so as to sustain conversations, maintain relationships, and build knowledge.

Notes

1 Allington, Richard (2002). What I've learned about effective reading instruction from a decade of studying exemplary elementary classroom teachers. *Phi Delta Kappan* (83) June 10, 740–747.

2 Applebee, Arthur N. (1996). *Curriculum as conversation: Transforming traditions of teaching and learning.* Chicago: University of Chicago Press.

3 Newmann, F. M., Marks, H. M., & Gamoran, A. (1996). Authentic pedagogy and student performance. *American Journal of Education, 104*(4), 280–312.

4 To craft a perspective and means for analysis, we need a language for talking about language. For most teachers, especially English language arts (ELA) teachers, that language is grammar and usage, with an emphasis on standard English conventions. ELA teachers refer to phrases, clauses, and parts of speech. They may teach figures of speech such as similes and metaphors. When assessing spoken language, they may correct subject–verb agreement, use of the "be" verb, and word endings. We are using a different way of describing language, one that comes from the fields of educational linguistics, literary theory, rhetoric and composition, anthropology, education, sociology, applied linguistics, and others (Rex, L. A. & Green, J. L. (2007). Classroom Discourse and Interaction: Reading across the traditions. In B. Spolsky & F. M. Hult (Eds.). *International handbook of educational linguistics* (pp. 571–584) London: Blackwell). It is an approach to language used to research teaching and learning in the fields of math, science, and social studies as well as English education. In any context in which people gather to conduct purposeful activity—families, businesses, hospitals, or churches—the ways of talking about talk we are presenting have been applied (e.g., Sarangi, S. & Roberts, C. (Eds.) (1999). *Talk, work and institutional order: Discourse in medical, mediation, and management settings.* Berlin: Mouton de Gruyter). In these applications, key terms, such as *identity* and *interaction*, reflect what to look at and how to analyze what is seen and heard.

5 James Gee: a scholar associated with New Literacy Studies (NLS). NLS is based on the view that reading and writing only make sense when studied in the context of social, cultural, historical, political, and economic practices of which they are only a part.

6 The term interdiscursivity is useful as a description of the complex relationships among discourses that inform what speakers say. Speakers have appropriated these discourses from sources they have encountered throughout their lifetimes. Every time someone says something it is influenced by multiple worlds and discourses and encounters multiple worlds and discourses. We may not be aware when we speak of the worlds of meaning that inform what we say. Nor are those with whom we speak aware of the worlds that inform their hearing of what we say. However, whenever there is an occasion that calls

for a spoken interaction, worlds will collide and intersect. At that moment speakers must decide how best to speak so as to achieve their purposes.

7   McCabe, M. (2006). *Enhancing face value: A description of teacher and student negotiation of power and politeness in a one-to-one first-grade reading intervention.* Unpublished dissertation. University of Michigan.

8   Alignment is a relational notion based upon speakers' and hearers' conceptions of what sort of person they take each other to be and what sort of intention they think each other is performing. The interaction realizes these beliefs as actual relations between participants. We take for granted that alignments exist prior to speaking and that alignments are jointly shaped during acts of conversing. Pre-existing frames, such as the roles and discourse practices of facilitators and participants and teachers and their students, are employed by people to create pedagogical talk. However, of more importance to us is the notion that the whole apparatus of the pedagogical discursive frame is immanent. It exists ready to be invoked by participants in any and all educational settings. In some ways, as the frame is invoked, elements are reproduced moment by moment in conversational action and carried through time. On the other hand, as current understandings of past and present conversations and in response to current circumstance, elements are also idiosyncratically reshaped.

9   Locher, M. (2004). *Power and politeness in action: Disagreements in oral communication.* Berlin: Mouton deGruyter.

10   We assume a view of learning that is social knowledge-building. It is the theory that informs how we explain power. We have found this view of social learning helpful for teaching in group settings such as classrooms and professional development communities. Our view builds on ideas from social constructivists, who have talked about how the individual learns as a member of a group (Steffe, L. P. & Gale, J. E. (1995). *Constructivism in education.* Mahwah, NJ: Erlbaum), and from social constructionists (Green, J. L. & Dixon, D. (1993). Introduction to talking knowledge into being: Discursive and social practices in classrooms. *Linguistics and education, 5*(3&4), 231–240), who explain how a group learns together. By adding discourse analysis to these ideas we can illustrate how both individuals and groups construct knowledge interactively through the ways people talk with each other. In other words, our approach views individual learning and collective learning in interdependent dynamic relationship. One cannot exist satisfactorily without the other. Individuals need to recognize how they can make use of the learning resources of the group. And, together, groups have to build and make recognizable those resources so individuals can satisfactorily engage in agentive ways so as to experience self-efficacy (e.g., Rex, L. A. & McEachen, D. (1999). "If anything is odd, inappropriate, confusing, or boring, it's probably important": The emergence of inclusive academic literacy through English classroom discussion practices. *Research in the teaching of English, 34*(1), 65–129; Rex, L. A. (2001). The remaking of a high school reader. *Reading Research Quarterly, 36*(3), 288–314).

11   Brown, P. & Levinson, S. (1987). *Politeness: Some universals in language usage.* Cambridge: Cambridge University Press.
      Goffman, E. (1967). *Interaction ritual: Essays on face-to-face behavior.* New York: Pantheon.
      O'Driscoll, J. (1996). About face: A defense and elaboration of universal dualism. *Journal of Pragmatics, 25*(1), 1–32.

12   Iles, Z. (1996). Collaborative repair in EFL classroom talk. *York Papers in Linguistics, 17,* 23–51.
      Liebscher, G., & Daileyocain, J. (2003). Conversational repair as a

role-defining mechanism in classroom interaction. *Modern Language Journal*, 87(3), 375–390.

13 This interpretation raises a concern with building understanding of teaching and learning through freeze-framing and the importance of carefully considering the advantages and disadvantages of working from single freeze-frame transcripts. The interpretations we make from brief snippets of interaction are trustworthy because they come from established ethnographically approached programs of research. Whether educators' interpretations can be trusted to guide further action will depend on how much additional evidence exists to bolster the trustworthiness of their interpretations. A single freeze-frame may initiate useful questions to ask, but rarely if ever provides solutions or answers for complicated issues.

14 Cohen, E. G., & Lotan, R. A. (1995). Producing equal-status interaction in the heterogeneous classroom. *American Educational Research Journal*, 32(1), 99–120.

15 Watts, R. (1991). *Power in family discourse*. Berlin: Mouton de Gruyter.

16 Throughout earlier chapters we have cautioned readers that interpreting transcripts without substantial contextual information is problematic. A reader's interpretation of this transcript without knowledge of Jack's classroom could easily produce a very different interpretation. By being a daily observer in this classroom and talking with each of the students who were part of this interaction, we can interpret the moves performed through these utterances in ways that the casual reader cannot. We emphasize this point so that readers will be sure to bring to their analyses the rich, contextual information that will make their interpretations trustworthy.

At what point can we trust contextual information? We accept our interpretations as valid because we conferred with the teachers and students in these interactions. Those people who are engaged in the interaction will have a point of view about what was occurring and will either agree or disagree with how they are represented. Like any good teacher when something happens in the classroom, you listen to the students' version and decide what is most plausible. The point to be made here is that single instances of talk are insufficient to support a trustworthy interpretation and we must be careful to put that single instance into the context of many interactions over longer periods of time.

17 Newmann, F. M., Secada, W. G., & Wehlage, G. G. (1995). *A guide to authentic instruction and assessment: Vision, standards and scoring*. Madison, WI: Wisconsin Center for Education Research.

18 Newmann, F. M., Marks, H. M., & Gamoran, A. (1996). Authentic pedagogy and student performance. *American Journal of Education*, 104(4), 280–312.

19 Rex, L. A. (Ed.) (2006). *Discourse of opportunity: How talk in learning situations creates and constrains*. Interactional Ethnographic Studies in Teaching and Learning. Cresskill, NJ: Hampton Press.

20 Lamb, S. M. (2000). Neuro-cognitive structure in the interplay of language and thought. In Martin Pütz and Marjolijn H. Verspoor (Eds.) *Explorations in linguistic relativity*. New York: John Benjamins. Also appears at http://www.ruf.rice.edu/~lamb/lt.htm

21 Agar, M. (1994). *Language shock: Understanding the culture of conversation*. New York: William Morrow.

22 Rex, L. A. (2003). Loss of the creature: The obscuring of inclusivity. *Communication Education*, 52(1), 30–46.

Rex, L. A. (2006). Acting "cool" and "appropriate": Toward a framework for considering literacy classroom interactions when race is a factor. *Journal of Literacy Research*, 38(3), 275–325.

Rex, L. A. & Nelson, M. (2004). How teachers' professional identities position high stakes test preparation in their classrooms. *Teachers College Record, 106*(6), 1288–1331.

23 For an illustration of membership categorization analysis see Rex, L. A. (2001). The remaking of a high school reader. *Reading Research Quarterly, 36*(3), 288–314.

24 Efforts by organizations such as Little People of America are being made to integrate people of small stature due to dwarfism into mainstream society. One effort involves replacing the various names by which people with dwarfism are referred to with "little people."

25 Rex, L. A., & Nelson, M. (2004). How teachers' professional identities position high stakes test preparation in their classrooms. *Teachers College Record, 106*(6), 1288–1331.

26 Meier, D. (2003). *In schools we trust*. Boston, MA: Beacon Press.

27 Davis, B., & Phelps, R. (2005). Exploring the common spaces of education and complexity: Transphenomenality, transdisciplinarity, and interdiscursivity. *Complicity: An International Journal of Complexity and Education, 2*(1), 1–4.

28 Guthrie, J. T. (2002). Preparing students for high stakes test taking in reading, In A. Farstrup, S. Samuels, & S. Jay (Eds.). *What research has to say about reading instruction* (3rd ed.). New York, DE: International Reading Association.

29 When the cultures of school differ in important ways from their home or neighborhood cultures, schools have been termed inequitably culturally incongruent for students. See, for example, Northwest Regional Education Laboratory (2001). *Advocating for culturally congruent school reform.* http://www.nwrac.org/congruent/index.html

30 Hillocks, G. (2002). *The testing trap: How state writing assessments control learning*. New York: Teachers College Press.
Gere, A., Christenbury, L., & Sassi, K. (2004). *Writing on-demand: Best practices and strategies for success.* Portsmouth, NH: Heinemann.

31 Barnes, D., Britton, J., & Rosen, H. (1969). *Language, the learner, and the school*. New York: Penguin.

32 For rich and useful guidance in teaching "on-demand" writing we recommend: Gere, A., Christenbury, L., & Sassi, K. (2005). *On-demand writing*. Portsmouth, NH: Heinemann.

33 We were impressed by Lucy Calkins' sensible recommendations to teachers for preparing students for tests: Calkins, L., Montgomery, K., Falk, B., & Santman, D. (1998). *A teacher's guide to standardized reading tests: Knowledge is power.* Portsmouth, NH: Heinemann.

34 Calkins, L. (1994). *The art of teaching writing*. Portsmouth, NH: Heinemann.

35 Oakland Schools. MEAPwriting—Genre study for MEAP Preparation. www.oakland.k12.mi.us/meapwriting

36 Hart, B., & Risley, T. (Spring, 2003). The early catastrophe: The 30 million word gap by age three. *American Educator.* http://www.aft.org/pubs-reports/american_educator/spring2003/catastrophe.html

37 Heath, S. B. (1983). *Ways with words: Language, life, and work in communities and classrooms.* Cambridge: Cambridge University Press.

38 Oakes, J. (1985). *Keeping track: How schools structure inequality.* New Haven, CT: Yale University Press.

39 Heath, S. B. (1983). *Ways with words: Language, life, and work in communities and classrooms.* Cambridge: Cambridge University Press.

Index